D0399367

STUDIES IN HISTORY, ECONOMICS AND PUBLIC LAW

Edited by the

**FACULTY OF POLITICAL SCIENCE
OF COLUMBIA UNIVERSITY**

NUMBER 370

INTERNATIONAL LAW IN NATIONAL COURTS

A STUDY OF THE ENFORCEMENT OF INTERNATIONAL LAW
IN GERMAN, SWISS, FRENCH AND BELGIAN COURTS

BY

RUTH D. MASTERS

INTERNATIONAL LAW IN NATIONAL COURTS

A Study of the Enforcement of International Law in
German, Swiss, French and Belgian Courts

BY

RUTH D. MASTERS

AMS PRESS
NEW YORK

COLUMBIA UNIVERSITY
STUDIES IN THE
SOCIAL SCIENCES

370

The Series was formerly known as
Studies in History, Economics and Public Law.

Reprinted with the permission of Columbia University Press
From the edition of 1932, New York
First AMS EDITION published 1968
Manufactured in the United States of America

Library of Congress Catalogue Card Number: 71-76631

AMS PRESS, INC.
NEW YORK, N. Y. 10003

To
THE OTHER TWO

CONTENTS

PART I

GERMANY

CHAPTER I

CHAPTER II

CHAPTER III

CHAPTER IV

CHAPTER V

CHAPTER VI

CHAPTER VII

PART II

SWITZERLAND

CHAPTER I

CHAPTER II

TABLE OF ABBREVIATIONS

9

S.   Sirey, *Recueil général des lois et des arrêts,* Paris, 1831–

Seuffert's *Archiv*   *Archiv für Entscheidungen der obersten Gerichte in den deutschen Staaten,* Munich, 1847–

ZPOR   *Zeitschrift für Internationales Privat- und Öffentliches Recht.* Leipzig, 1903-1909; vols. 12-19 (formerly Böhm, *Zeitschrift für Internationales Privat- und Strafrecht,* Leipzig, 1891-1902; continued as *Niemeyer's Zeitschrift für Internationales Recht,* Leipzig, 1910–

Z. V.   *Zeitschrift für Völkerrecht,* Breslau, 1908–

INTRODUCTION

THE relation between international law and the municipal law of states is at present one of the most controversial and widely discussed subjects among continental European—especially German, Austrian and Italian—jurists. In general it may be said that the question is regarded as principally a theoretical one which depends, in the last analysis, on the writer's concept of the nature and authority of international law. For the judge of a municipal court, however, the antithesis between international law and municipal law takes the form of the purely practical question: Is this court bound to apply the rules of international law?

This practical aspect of the relation between international law and municipal law, namely, the enforcement of the former in municipal courts, has been neglected to a certain extent in the discussions of continental European writers. It is clear that the position of international law in the courts can not be established by theories, but requires a minute examination of the practice of the courts in actual cases. Such an examination has been attempted in this study for the courts of Germany, Switzerland, France and Belgium.

A discussion of the views of outstanding writers on the relation between international law and municipal law would undoubtedly prove to be of interest as an introduction to the subsequent description of the practice of the courts in these four countries. It would, however, constitute a treatise by itself and exceeds the scope of this study.[1]

---

[1] The whole *status causae et controversiae* is ably set forth by Kunz, " *Landesrecht und Völkerrecht* " in Strupp's *Wörterbuch des Völkerrechts* (1924), vol. i, pp. 788 *et seq*. See also Verdross in *Recueil des cours de l'Académie de droit international de la Haye* (hereafter cited as

Nevertheless, as it is certain that the doctrines of writers of

Recueil), vol. xvi (1927), pp. 251 *et seq.* Strupp, *Éléments de Droit International Public, Universel, Européen et Américain* (Paris, 1930) summarizes the present theories on the relation of international law to municipal law as follows (p. 21) :

A. " Dualist " theories :

Triepel, *Recueil*, vol. vii, pp. 7 *et seq.*
[see also: *Völkerrecht und Landesrecht* (Leipzig, 1899)].
Strupp, *op. cit.*, pp. 19-21.
Anzilotti, *Corso di diritto internazionale* (Rome, 1912), vol. i, p. 50; *Cour de droit international* (Paris, 1929), p. 51; *Rivista di diritto internazionale*, vol. i, pp. 45 *et seq.*
Heilborn, *Grundbegriffe des Völkerrechts* (Stuttgart, 1912), p. 13.
Cavaglieri, *Corso [Lezioni?] di diritto internazionale* (Naples, 1925), vol. i, pp. 20, 25.
Gemma, *Appunti di diritto internazionale* (Bologna, 1923), p. 9.
Liszt-Fleischmann, *Das Völkerrecht systematisch dargestellt* (Berlin, 1925), p. 14.

B. " Monist " theories :

I. Supremacy of municipal law :

(a) International law as " external public law ".
The so-called " *Bonner Schule* ", viz. :
P. Zorn, *Staatsrecht des Deutschen Reiches* (Berlin, 1895-97), p. 493 [see also: A. Zorn, *Grundzüge des Völkerrechts* (Leipzig, 1903), p. 7].
E. Kaufmann, *Das Wesen des Völkerrechts und die clausula rebus sic stantibus* (Tübingen, 1911), pp. 159, 179, 190 *et seq.*
Wenzel, *Juristische Grundprobleme* (Berlin, 1920), pp. 356 *et seq.*, 403.
(b) Theory of " auto-limitation ".
Bergbohm, *Staatsverträge und Gesetze als Quellen des Völkerrechts* (Dorpat, 1876).
Jellinek, *Die rechtliche Natur der Staatenverträge* (Wien, 1880).

II. Choice between supremacy of municipal law and supremacy of international law :

Kelsen, *Das Problem der Souveränitat und die Theorie des Völkerrechts* (Tübingen, 1920) ; *Der soziologische und der juristische Staatsbegriff* (Tübingen, 1928).
A. Merkl, *Die Lehre von der Rechtskraft* (Leipzig, 1923).

repute exert a certain influence on judges—especially judges of the same nationality as the writers—it will prove helpful for an understanding of the attitude of the courts, if we briefly explain the two principal theories on the relation between international law and municipal law, and their bearing on the question whether municipal courts are bound to apply rules of international law. As their chief exponents on the continent of Europe, W. Kaufmann and H. Triepel have been chosen; Kaufman, representing the so-called " monist " theory, based on the supremacy of international law, and Triepel, the principal representative of the " dualist " theory.[2]

III. Supremacy of international law:

    (a) Old and new Naturalist doctrines.

    (b) With divergences the following:

        v. Bar, *Archiv für Rechts und Wirtschaftsphilosophie*, vol. vi, p. 145.

        Lansing, *Notes on Sovereignty* (Washington, 1921).

        W. Kaufmann, *Die Rechtskraft des internationalen Rechts und das Verhältnis der Staatsgesetzgebung und der Staatsorgane zu demselben* (Stuttgart, 1899).

        Krabbe, *Die moderne Staatsidee* (Haag, 1919).

        Duguit, *Traité de droit constitutionnel* (Paris, 1921-25), vol. i, p. 550.

        Salvioli, *Rivista di diritto internazionale*, vol. xiv (1921), p. 20.

    (c) The Viennese School:

        Kelsen, *Das Problem der Souveränitat und die Theorie des Völkerrechts* (Tübingen, 1920), p. 204. *Recueil*, vol. iv (1926), pp. 231 *et seq.*

        Verdross, *Die Einheit des rechtlichen Weltbildes* (Tübingen, 1923); *Die Verfassung der Völkerrechtsgemeinschaft* (Berlin, 1926); *Recueil*, vol. xvi (1927), pp. 287 *et seq.*

        Kunz, *op. cit.*

        Wittmayer in Z. V., vol. xiii (1924), p. I.

        Scelle in RGDP, vol. v (1923), pp. 116 *et seq.*

        Cavaglieri in *Rivista di diritto internazionale*, vol. iii, pp. 188 *et seq.*

[2] W. Kaufmann, *Die Rechtskraft des internationalen Rechts und das*

Kaufmann maintains that international law and municipal law are parts of a single legal system in which international law is the higher law. His theory is most clearly evident in his views regarding conflicts between treaties and subsequent municipal laws. Because international law is superior to municipal law, and because it is immediately binding on persons and courts, he claims that international law cannot be overruled by a subsequent municipal law,[3] and that, therefore, the courts must disregard the municipal law and apply the treaty. Kaufmann admits, however, that such has not been the practice of the courts.[4][5]

Triepel, on the other hand, regards international law and municipal law as two separate legal systems for the reason that they have different sources and address themselves to different subjects. International law, says Triepel, has its source in the common consent of states, members of the

Verhältnis der Staatsgesetzgebung und der Staatsorgane zu demselben (Stuttgart, 1899); H. Triepel, *Völkerrecht und Landesrecht* (Leipzig, 1899). In "*Zur Konstruktion des Völkerrechts*", Z. V., vol. viii (1914), Verdross coined the terms "monist" and "dualist" theories on the relation between international law and municipal law; the former to apply to such theories as regarded international and municipal law as parts of a single legal system, the latter to apply to such theories as regarded the two as separate systems, especially to Triepel's theory. The terms have been generally accepted and are freely used.

[3] Kaufmann, *op. cit.*, p. 78.

[4] *Ibid.*, p. 73.

[5] Since the war, the so-called "Viennese School"—Kelsen and Verdross, chiefly—have with most ingenious and brilliant arguments attempted to prove the unity of all law. International law and municipal law are envisaged as parts of one legal system in which every legal norm depends on another, higher legal norm, until, at the very top of the whole structure the maxim *pacta sunt servanda* is reached which, in the opinion of Kelsen and Verdross, is the fundamental legal norm (in the view of Kelsen the fundamental hypothesis!) on which every other legal norm, both of international law and of municipal law depends. Kelsen and Verdross argue that since *pacta sunt servanda* is a rule of international law, international law is superior to municipal law.

society of states; this consent may be given expressly—conventional international law—or impliedly—customary international law. The subjects of international law are the states; private persons are often objects of international law, e. g. when their rights and obligations are regulated by international law, but they are never its subjects in the sense that international law addresses itself directly to them. Municipal law, on the other hand, has its source in the command of the state or in custom which has grown up within the state; its subjects are private persons, viz. all persons subject to the jurisdiction of the state.

International law and municipal law then are two separate legal systems; consequently, the laws of one have *ipso jure* no force in the other. Triepel regards international law as the higher of the two, because it has its source in the combined will of all or a great many states, while municipal law has its source in the will of one state only. Nevertheless, since the two legal systems are separate, international law does not *ipso jure* overrule municipal law in a municipal court. The important point in Triepel's theory is that he draws a distinction between the relation of international law to municipal law for the state, i. e. in the sphere of international law, and for a municipal court, i. e. in the sphere of municipal law. A state cannot escape an international obligation by pleading that its own municipal law prevents it from fulfilling this obligation; the latter has no force in the sphere of international law. Conversely, for municipal courts and private persons, municipal law alone is obligatory and international law only in so far as it has been adopted by the state into its own law. International law has no force in the sphere of municipal law. In order to fulfill those international obligations which require to be carried out within states, every state must, as Triepel says, *transform* them into municipal laws. They are then enforced by municipal courts as part of the law of the land.

According to Kaufmann, enforcement of international law through a municipal court signifies that the court has applied rules of international law; according to Triepel, that the court has applied rules of municipal law which have incorporated rules of international law.

It may be objected that this distinction between international law and international law transformed into municipal law is specious. However, it enables Triepel to explain why international law which—being a law created by many states—is superior to municipal law (the law of one state only), nevertheless, does not have force superior to municipal law in municipal courts. It is there equal to municipal law, because, says Triepel, it has by an act of the state been transformed into municipal law and is applied by the courts not as international law but as municipal law.

The influence of these two principal theories, especially of Triepel's so-called " dualist " theory, on the courts will appear in the following chapters.

The study is limited to the enforcement of international law through the courts of Germany, Switzerland, France and Belgium. Reference will occasionally be made to Anglo-American practice for purposes of comparison, without, however, going into a thorough examination of the practice of British and American courts.[6]

No discussion of the position of international law in prize

---

[6] The enforcement of international law in British and American courts is discussed by Picciotto, *The Relation of International Law to the Law of England and of the United States of America* (London, 1915); Wright, *The Enforcement of International Law through Municipal Law in the United States* (Urbana, 1916), and articles in the *American Journal of International Law*, vol. x, pp. 706 *et seq.*; vol. xi, pp. 1 *et seq.*, and vol. xvii, pp. 234 *et seq.*; Holland, *Studies in International Law* (Oxford, 1898), pp. 176 *et seq.*; Scott, *Legal Nature of International Law, American Journal of International Law*, vol. i, pp. 831 *et seq.*; Willoughby, *Legal Nature of International Law, ibid.*, vol. ii, pp. 357 *et seq.*; Potter, *ibid.*, vol. xix, pp. 315 *et seq.*

courts will be included; the subject has already been fully covered by Garner [7] and Verzijl.[8]

The two chief difficulties in seeking to state accurately in what manner and to what degree the courts of these four countries enforce international law are, first, that the courts rarely discuss the reasons why rules of customary international law are obligatory on them; in the majority of cases they do not seem to be conscious of the existence of an antithesis between international and municipal law. Second, the courts of all four countries are guilty of carelessness in the use of the term " international law "; in fact, it must be stated that not one case could be found which could compare favorably with Lord Alverstone's opinion in *West Rand Central Gold Mining Co. v. the King* [9] with respect to clarity of expression and exact definition of the court's understanding of the term " international law ".

The courts usually give with a fair degree of precision the reasons why they enforce treaties, but when enforcing customary international law, they occasionally employ such terms as " German international law " [10] or " French international law ".[11] The courts frequently declare that a rule is applicable, because it is " generally recognized ". With the exception of the German courts since 1919, the courts do not explain what they understand by " generally recognized rules of international law ", especially whether they require that a rule of international law, to be enforceable by them, must have been accepted by their country.

[7] Garner, *Prize Law during the World War* (New York, 1927), pp. 142-203.

[8] Verzijl, *Droit des Prises de la Grande Guerre* (Leyden, 1924), pp. 72-156.

[9] L. R. [1915] 2 K. B., 391.

[10] See RGZ 85, 375, 376; *infra*, p. 38.

[11] See D.1859.1.327; *infra*, p. 144.

The second difficulty is, as we have said, the uncertainty as to what the courts understand by the term " international law ". A comparison of the definitions of this word by various authorities on international law shows that it is given a wider meaning by some than by others. Generally speaking, we may say that Anglo-American writers give the name international law to those rules only which have been accepted by all, or almost all states, while continental European writers usually define international law as the body of all those rules which are obligatory on two or several states in their relation with one another.[12]

To a strict positivist, international law consists of rules which have been accepted by every state which is to be bound by them. The process is naturally a gradual one, so that a given rule passes from the stage when it is accepted by two states over the stage when it is accepted by the majority of states to the final one when it is accepted by all states. Should it be said that it is a rule of international law only when it has reached the last stage? Or when it has received the assent of a great number of states, i. e. when it is " generally recognized "? The latter is the Anglo-American view.

The continental European point of view is best expressed by Oppenheim, who may be cited here as a representative of the continent rather than of England, having been born and educated in Germany and received his legal training in German universities. He says:

[12] Compare Hall, *International Law* (Oxford, 1924), p. 12; Hyde, *International Law* (Boston, 1922), p. 4; Hershey, *The Essentials of International Public Law and Organization* (New York, 1927), p. 1, especially note 1, with Oppenheim, *International Law* (London, 1928), 4th ed., p. 3; Hatscheck, *Völkerrecht als System rechtlich bedeutsamer Staatsakte* (Leipzig, 1923), p. 5; Strupp, *Grundzüge des positiven Völkerrechts* (Bonn, 1926), p. 1; Liszt-Fleischmann, *Das Völkerrecht* (Berlin, 1925), p. 12; Anzilotti, *Lehrbuch des Völkerrechts* (Berlin, 1929), p. 66.

Law of nations or international law is the name for the body of customary and conventional rules which are considered legally binding by civilised states in their intercourse with each other. Such part of these rules as is binding upon all the civilised states without exception as, for instance, the law connected with legation and treaties, is called *universal* international law, in contradistinction to *particular* international law which is binding on two or a few states only. But it is also necessary to distinguish *general* international law. This name must be given to the body of such rules as are binding upon a great many states, including leading powers.[13]

Most Anglo-American writers limit the term " international law " to what continental European writers usually call " general international law ".[14] In view of this discrepancy in the definition of this word, it has been found advisable to state at the outset what meaning will be given to the word international law in this study.

Since we are here dealing with continental European states, the wider definition of the term is accepted. Whenever the term " international law " is used in the text, it is to be understood in the sense attributed to it by Strupp, viz. that it is " the body of legal rules which regulate the rights and duties of two or several states, subjects of international law." [15]

This study then deals with the enforcement of particular, general and universal, customary and conventional international law in the courts of Germany, Switzerland, France and Belgium.

[13] Oppenheim, *op. cit.*, p. 3.

[14] Of course, Anglo-American writers admit the existence of a conventional international law which is obligatory on the states which have accepted it, but although such conventional international law is acknowledged to be international law for the states bound by it, it is not generally included in the term "international law".

[15] Strupp, *op. cit.*, p. 1.

PART I

GERMANY

CHAPTER I

INTRODUCTION

SINCE the latter part of the 19th century the majority of German writers have been positivists; they maintained that international law was a *jus inter gentes* in the strictest sense, whose subjects were states only and never individuals. Heilborn, for example, says: " The law of nations is neither a legal system for the relations between individuals, nor for the relation between individual and state . . . the dominant and almost unanimous opinion is that the law of nations is a legal system for states only." [1]

After the appearance of Triepel's treatise *Völkerrecht und Landesrecht,* most German writers accepted the " dualist " theory of the relation of international law and municipal law, which remained practically unchallenged until the advent of the so-called " Viennese School " after the war.[2] At present, " dualists " and " monists " are engaged in a heated controversy over the antithesis between international law and municipal law. It will be seen later in this chapter that the German courts adhere to the " dualist " theory.

Triepel's classical book which appeared in 1899 was the first systematic study of the relation between international law and municipal law ever attempted. The basic principles of his theory have been briefly stated in the previous chapter.

As has been said before, the important point in Triepel's theory is that he regards international law as a law superior to municipal law, but maintains that the former is, nevertheless, not *eo ipso* obligatory on municipal courts; the reason being that international law and municipal law are separate

---

[1] Heilborn, *Grundbegriffe des Völkerrechts* (Stuttgart, 1912), p. 13.
[2] See *supra,* p. 10.

legal systems.   International law, therefore, must be transformed into municipal law by each state, in order to be binding on its courts and persons subject to its jurisdiction.
Municipal courts never apply international law proper, but
always municipal law by which the international obligations
of the state are carried into effect.

Closely related to, but probably more widely known than
Triepel's theory is the so-called Laband-Gneist theory on
treaties.   In view of the influence which the latter has had
even outside Germany, it may be well to briefly state its basic
principles.   Laband and Gneist maintained that a treaty
could be valid in international law and obligatory on the
states which had ratified it, and yet be unenforceable in the
courts of these states; in order to render the treaty binding
on the agents of the state, notably the courts, and on persons
subject to its jurisdiction, each state had to declare that the
treaty should have effect internally also.   In other words,
Laband and Gneist distinguished between the international
validity of treaties and their obligatory force in municipal
law and made the latter dependent on an act of the state
which in effect transformed the international contract into
an internal law.   This transformation of the treaty into a
municipal law could take place in various ways: a state could
pass a law embodying the provisions of the treaty, or a custom could have grown up in a state that treaties are to be
published or promulgated in like manner as laws and are
thereupon binding on the agents of the state and private
persons subject to its jurisdiction.   In every case, however,
an act of the state had to intervene after exchange of ratifications, by which the treaty was rendered obligatory on
persons within the state.   To quote Laband:

It is an opinion held by many that the agents of a state are bound
by international law to execute the provisions of treaties, and
that international law as a higher source of law than the public

law of states could have this binding force; this view is, however, based on a misconception of the nature of international law. International law can only create law between states but never within a state; it can be only an indirect source of municipal law.[3]

The gist of the "dualist" theory then is that municipal courts do not enforce rules of customary international law and treaties in their character as international law, but apply them as part of the municipal law of their state, after they have been adopted into the law of the land by an act of the state. On principle they are, in municipal courts, equal to other municipal laws, i. e. they overrule earlier and are superseded by later laws.

The "dualists" admit that a state commits an internationally illegal act when it passes a law violating a rule of customary international law or an existing treaty. Nevertheless, owing to the separation of the two legal systems, international law and municipal law, the later law would be obligatory on municipal courts. Because of the international consequences which such a law would have for the state, however, the "dualists" maintain that courts interpret laws with the presumption that no violation of international law has been intended by the legislator. To quote Heilborn:

Because the state is the creator of municipal law and, at the same time, co-creator of that part of international law which is binding on it, it follows that it is responsible for a material harmony between the two. . . . In interpreting municipal laws, it is therefore to be presumed that the state did not intend a conflict with international law. . . . If it is impossible to avoid a conflict, however, the judge and the other agents of the state must obey the municipal law.[3]

[3] Laband, *Deutsches Staatsrecht* (Tübingen, 1911), p. 166. See also Gneist, *Gutachten über die Auslegung des Paragraph 48 der Verfassungsurkunde*, annex in E. Meier, *Über den Abschluss von Staatsverträgen* (Leipzig, 1874).

[4] Heilborn, *Grundbegriffe und Geschichte des Völkerrechts* (Stuttgart, 1912), pp. 89, 91.

And Triepel says:

Our theory calls for a restrictive interpretation of such municipal laws which, if literally taken, would lead to the conclusion that they violate international law. Because, according to a true and sound principle, the presumption must be repudiated that a legislator intends to escape his obligations in international law by enacting a statute—unless the spirit of the law imperatively demands this interpretation. In the latter case, however, the judge is bound to apply the law that violates international law.[5]

We shall now proceed to examine in what manner international law is enforced in German courts. We shall first study the position of treaties and customary international law in the courts of the Empire [6] i. e. during the period 1871-1919; we shall then discuss article 4 of the Republican constitution of Aug. 11, 1919 which declares that " The generally [allgemein] recognized rules of international law are deemed to form an integral part of German federal law "; and finally the position of treaties and customary international law in the courts of the Republic.

This plan has been adopted chiefly for the reason that it affords the best means of observing the practical value and effect of the much-debated article 4 of the Republican constitution. The discussion of cases dealing with questions of international law before 1919 will furnish the necessary background for an understanding of the intentions of the framers of article 4, and the subsequent examination of the practice of the Republican courts will show how far these intentions have been realized.

[5] Triepel, *op. cit.*, pp. 398-399.

[6] The term " Empire " is used whenever reference is made to Germany during the period 1871-1919, the term " Republic " when the reference is to Germany since 1919. The term " Reich " is employed to designate the German state as a political entity since 1871.

CHAPTER II

TREATIES 1871-1919

ACCORDING to article 11 of the constitution of 1871 treaties are concluded by the emperor, but " treaties with foreign states relating to any of the subjects which belong to the sphere of federal legislation, according to article 4 [of the constitution], require for their conclusion the consent of the *Bundesrat* and for their validity the acceptance of the *Reichstag* ".[1]

Section 3 of article 11 has given rise to much discussion: does it make the consent of *Bundesrat* and *Reichstag* a *condicio juris* for the international validity of treaties dealing with matters reserved by article 4 of the constitution to the legislature of the " Reich ", or does it merely make the *execution* of such treaties dependent on approval of the legislature, i. e. does the obligatory force of treaties in German municipal law alone depend on the consent of *Bundesrat* and *Reichstag;* or, finally, is the consent of the *Bundesrat* required for the international validity of such treaties, and that of the *Reichstag* for their internal enforcement?

Laband and Gneist took the second view and the majority

[1] *Bundesrat* and *Reichstag* were the two houses of the legislature; the former representing the German states, the latter the German people. The German text of the quoted passage, which is section 3 of article ii, reads as follows : " *Insoweit die Verträge mit fremden Staaten sich auf solche Gegenstände beziehen, welche nach Artikel 4 in den Bereich der Reichsgesetzgebung gehören, ist zu ihrem Abschluss die Zustimmung des Bundesrates und zu ihrer Gültigkeit die Genehmigung des Reichstages erforderlich.*"

of German writers have followed them.   As a matter of fact,
however, the approval of the legislature was regularly
obtained before the treaty was ratified by the emperor.[2]   It
is not clear whether this practice was due to a belief on the
part of the government that legislative approval was required
to bind Germany in international law, or whether the government wanted to avoid the danger that a treaty, which had become obligatory on Germany might fail to receive legislative
assent to render it enforceable in German courts.   At any
rate, this assent was regularly obtained before the treaty
became internationally binding, and the treaty was then published immediately in the *Reichsgesetzblatt,* the legal gazette
in which laws had to be published in order to become obligatory on persons within Germany.   The treaty was thereupon
regarded by the courts as equivalent to a federal statute.

In the case of *Böhm,* the *Reichsgericht* [3] said, with respect
to the treaty with Great Britain of 1872 :

The treaty is, of course, not a statute in name, but it is a statute
in fact; at any rate, article 7 of the treaty constitutes a binding
legal norm which contains an important rule of procedure. . . .
The treaty was signed by order of H. M. the Emperor, thereupon submitted to the *Reichstag* for confirmation in accordance
with the constitution, approved by the latter and referred to
the *Bundesrat.*   The treaty was then ratified by the Emperor
and published in the *Reichsgesetzblatt.* . . . The treaty was,
therefore, concluded in accordance with article 11, section 3 of

[2] See v. Rönne, *Das Verfassungsrecht des Deutschen Reiches* (Leipzig,
1892), p. 61.

[3] This is the highest German court, a federal court, instituted by the
law of April 11, 1877, with seat in Leipzig.   Its members were appointed
by the emperor upon recommendation by the *Bundesrat*; the number of
so-called " *Senate* ", i. e. chambers, was fixed by the German chancellor.
It was opened Oct. 1, 1879 with a membership consisting of one president,
seven presidents of chambers and 60 judges.   The membership has since
been increased.   The court hears civil and criminal cases on appeal from
the state courts of last resort.

the constitution. . . . It fulfills, at the same time, the conditions which article 5 of the constitution lays down for the passage of a statute, and by publication in the legal gazette it has obtained force of law for everybody, especially for the agents of the state.[4]

The court regarded the treaty as having, upon publication in the *Reichsgesetzblatt,* obtained force equal to that of a federal statute.

In a case which involved the patent rights of a Frenchman under the Paris Convention for the Protection of Industrial Property of 1883, the same court made the following statement:

The accession of Germany to the Convention of Paris . . . was deposited with the Swiss government March 21, 1903 and the convention has, therefore, become internationally binding on Germany (as of May 1, 1903), according to article 11, section 1 of the constitution. In order to make the convention effective within Germany, the consent of *Bundesrat* and *Reichstag* had to be obtained, in accordance with article 11, section 3 of the constitution. The consent of the *Bundesrat* was given May 9, 1901, that of the *Reichstag* May 15, 1901, and the convention was then published in the *Reichsgesetzblatt* on April 9, 1903. *The convention has thus become a federal law and has been incorporated into German legislation on trade and commerce.*[5]

In its decision of Sept. 22, 1885, the *Reichsgericht* stated why it was bound by treaties which had received legislative approval and had been published. It said:

Although international treaties are said to lack force of law [i. e. force of law *within* the state] on account of their con-

[4] Decision of Apr. 17, 1879; cited in Goltdammer's *Archiv*, vol. 27, p. 387.

[5] Case of *H. H. v. L. Ch. in Paris* (cited as the *Patent case*) ; decision of Oct. 26, 1914; RGZ 85, 375, 377. (Italics inserted.)

tractual nature, they are, nevertheless, possessed of legal force in all states where they have been made laws, in accordance with the constitutional requirements for the passage of statutes; in their nature as statutes they bind citizens and agents of the state, as well as the state itself.[6]

In its decision of Aug. 29, 1888 the *Reichsgericht* stated that the provisions of the extradition treaty between Prussia and the Netherlands of November 17, 1850 were obligatory on it, "since the treaty . . . must, according to articles 45, 48 and 106 of the Prussian constitution of Jan. 31, 1850, be regarded as having force of law in Prussia ".[6a]

As was pointed out in the *Böhm* case, treaties which have received legislative approval and which have been published in the *Reichsgesetzblatt* fulfill the requirements of article 5 of the constitution with regard to the passage of statutes.[7] The *Reichsgericht* said in an extradition case dealing with the legal force of the extradition treaty with Belgium that treaties are binding on the courts *because* they have the force of federal statutes.   " Because extradition treaties are in Germany published in the form of statutes, they are binding also on the courts which have jurisdiction over the extradited persons ".[8]

In the case *Gebrüder T. v. Mecklenburgischen Fiskus,* the same court held that a state may by treaty undertake certain obligations towards its own nationals which, after publica-

[6] Case *v. S.*; RGStr. 12, 281, 384. See in the same sense: *National Cash Register Co. v. Sch.*, RGZ 72, 242.

[6a] Case of *v. D.*; Goldtdammer's *Archiv*, vol. 37, p. 404. See also the decision of the same court of May 24, 1910 (case of *v. G.*; RGStr. 43, 420) where it was held that the boundary treaty between Prussia and the Netherlands of Oct. 7, 1816 had the force of a Prussian law and bound the judge.

[7] See *supra*, p. 29.

[8] Case of *v. K.* Decision of May 5, 1908; RGStr. 41, 272, 275. See also decision of *Reichsgericht* of Dec. 8, 1913; RGStr. 48, 26, 30.

tion of the treaty, become part of the public law of the state. In this case suit was brought against the state of Mecklenburg-Schwerin for the payment of damages caused to the plaintiff's ship in the river Elbe. It was claimed that the state had neglected to remove obstructions in the navigable channel of the river Elbe and had, therefore, violated its obligations under the international convention for the régime of the river Elbe, the *Elbschiffahrtsakte* of 1821 and the *Additionalakte* of 1844. Mecklenburg-Schwerin had ratified and published these two treaties. The plaintiff argued that they had therefore become part of the public law of the state. The *Reichsgericht* said:

The plaintiff has no contractual right in the preservation of the channel; his claim for damages would be well founded only if the defendant were obliged by a legal norm to remove obstructions from the bed of the river. . . . *There exists no doubt that such a legal norm could be contained in a published treaty and that a state may, by publishing the treaty, create a prescription of public law by which it binds itself, towards all persons interested, to perform certain acts* . . . such an obligation of the state may be of a nature that it is made liable for any damage caused by a culpable omission of measures required for the fulfillment of this obligation.[9]

The court admitted that if the state had in the treaty bound itself towards private persons to keep the channel of the river Elbe navigable, the suit would have been allowed. But, in this instance, the court denied that such an obligation had been undertaken by the contracting states. It held, on the contrary, that in the treaties the contracting states had merely accepted obligations towards each other, and not towards private persons. The violations of the treaty by one of the states that had ratified it, made that state liable in damages

[9] Decision of Oct. 8, 1895; RGZ 36, 183 (italics inserted).

to the other contracting states, but not to private persons. The court said: " The claim must be rejected, because the treaties in question must be interpreted to have created obligations between the contracting states only and not towards every person interested in the matter." [10]

The cases cited show that treaties are enforced by the *Reichsgericht* as part of German municipal law; they are deemed to have become federal laws upon publication in the *Reichsgesetzblatt*. However, whenever treaties regulate the conduct of states as entities in their relation with each other, the court does not consider that they have, through publication, become part of the municipal law. Now it is, of course, true that treaties always contain obligations of the contracting states towards each other only. The court apparently wishes to distinguish between obligations which in their practical effects determine the conduct of the states towards each other, and those which determine the conduct of the states towards private persons; in other words, treaties whose object is the regulation of the conduct of the contracting states towards each other, and treaties whose objects are also rights and obligations of private persons.[11]

The question whether the courts were bound to apply municipal laws which conflicted with previously concluded treaties assumed importance after the passage of the great law codes in the last quarter of the 19th century. After Germany's unification in 1871, the whole domain of civil, criminal, commercial and military law, with the exception of a limited number of matters of special local interest which continued to be regulated by the states, was delegated to the control of the federal legislature. The laws of the Reich were collected and unified in codes. Some of these codes contained provisions conflicting with treaties which the

[10] *Ibid.*, p. 184.
[11] See RGZ 121, 7; *infra*, p. 69.

German states and the North German Confederation had previously concluded with foreign states. The treaties of the North German Confederation were taken over by the Empire and, since they had been published, were regarded as equivalent to federal statutes. The treaties of the several German states remained in force, unless they were terminated by mutual agreement of the contracting states. Having been published in the states, they had force equal to state laws. Most of the codes provided that earlier state laws which conflicted with the new codes were annulled. In a number of cases the courts had to decide whether the codes overruled earlier treaties which the North German Confederation and the several German states had concluded with foreign states and which had remained internationally binding on Germany or German states.

The position taken by the German legislature towards this question is best expressed in the record of the proceedings of the legislative committee which drafted the civil code.[12] It had been proposed in committee to include in the introductory law to the civil code an article stating: " The provisions of the treaties which the Reich has concluded with a foreign state, remain in force ". This article corresponded to article 56 of the introductory law which stated: " The provisions of treaties which a state [member state of the Reich] has concluded with foreign powers prior to the coming into force of the civil code remain in force." In article 55 of the introductory law it was declared that state laws conflicting with the civil code are annulled unless otherwise provided in the civil code itself.

The article declaring that the treaties of the Reich remain in force was not accepted by the committee, in view of the following considerations:

[12] *Protokolle der Kommission für die zweite Lesung des Entwurfs des BGB* (Berlin, 1899), vol. vi.

Treaties obtain their obligatory force within the state and thereby the character of objective law only through their publication as statutes and can, regardless of their binding force on the state in international law, be divested of this character by a subsequent statute. As long as the treaty remains in force in regard to the foreign state, however, it is not to be presumed that the legislator intended the statute to do this [i. e. annul the obligatory force of the treaty within the state].[12a]

The committee was of the opinion that these considerations were sufficient to prevent a misinterpretation of the civil code and that it was, therefore, unnecessary to state expressly that no violation of existing treaties of the Reich was intended with the civil code.

It was held, however, that the inclusion of article 56 in the introductory law was necessary. The following reasons were given:

It is different with treaties which a state [member state of the Reich] has concluded with a foreign state, because these treaties would, in their nature as state laws, . . . be annulled by the code. For this reason it was deemed necessary to include a statement declaring that these treaties remained in force, whereas the fact that treaties of the Reich continued in force was to be concluded from the intentions with which the new codes were enacted.[13]

The legislature took it for granted that the civil code would not be interpreted as having intended to overrule existing treaties of the Reich. Similar statements were made by it in regard to most of the other codes; for example, with regard to the bankruptcy law: " It is self-evident that . . . it is not intended to interfere with existing or future

[12a] *Protokolle der Kommission für die zweite Lesung des Entwurfs des BGB* (Berlin, 1899), vol. vi, p. 563.

[13] *Protokolle der Kommission für die zweite Lesung des Entwurfs des BGB* (Berlin, 1899), vol. vi, p. 563.

treaties." [14]   And with regard to the code of civil procedure: "The provisions of treaties with foreign states remain, of course, in force." [15]

The legislature had thus clearly stated that it did not intend to violate treaty obligations. The *Reichsgericht* consistently interpreted statutes with the presumption that they had not been intended to overrule previously concluded treaties. In its decision of Dec. 17, 1880, the court said, in connection with a conflict between the trademark law of 1874 and the treaty with Spain of March 30, 1868: " It was not the intention of the legislator and is not expressed in his words that the international obligations of the Reich towards other powers were to be suspended . . . or in any way modified ".[16]

In a case dealing with the conflict between the treaty with Russia of 1874 and certain provisions of the code of civil procedure, the same court said: " Treaties are regularly not affected by the legislation of one of the contracting states ".[17]

In a later case dealing with the same treaty, the *Reichsgericht* referred to the statements made in the legislative committee which had drafted the civil code, in connection with the proposal of an article stating that treaties of the

[14] *Motive zu dem Entwurf einer Konkursordnung und dem Entwurf eines Einführungsgesetzes*; document for no. 200 in *Stenographische Berichte über die Verhandlungen des deutschen Reichstages*. (Second legislative session) II. Session 1874–1875, vol. iv, *Anlagen zu den Verhandlungen des Reichstages* (Berlin, 1875), p. 1376.

[15] *Begründung des Entwurfs einer Zivilprozessordnung und des Einführungsgesetzes*; document for no. 6 in *Stenographische Berichte über die Verhandlungen des deutschen Reichstages* (second legislative session). II. Session 1874–1875), vol. iii, *Anlagen zu den Verhandlungen des Reichstags* (Berlin, 1875), p. 559. See also Walz, *Die Abänderung völkerrechtsgemässen Landesrechts* (Berlin, 1927), pp. 56-62.

[16] Case *v. I.*; RGStr. 3, 127, 129.

[17] Case *v. H. v. Sp. und Genossen*; decision of June 23, 1890; RGZ 26, 117, 128.

Reich remain untouched by the new code. The court said that this proposal had been rejected " because it was considered to be self-evident that treaties which had once obtained the force of objective law could, of course, be repealed by a later statute, but that such an intention was not to be presumed as long as the treaty remained in force ".[18]

In the case of *Bräg,* the court declared that, on principle, treaties could be abrogated by a later law:

Treaties relating to matters of internal legislation are—with respect to their validity as German laws—subject to the general rules applicable to German federal laws. They can therefore—apart from the question of the international consequences to the state—be overruled by legislation.[19]

In this case, however, there existed no conflict between treaty and law.

In a case decided July 1, 1889, the *Reichsgericht* said that it was not to be presumed that the legislature had intended to overrule the treaty between Saxony and Austria of 1854 when enacting the federal bankruptcy law:

Legal norms which are contained in treaties do not rest, as do state laws, on an order of the legislative power, but are created by the union of the wills of the contracting states; they can, therefore, as a rule be abrogated by mutual consent of the contracting parties only. The unilateral abrogation of a treaty would violate the rights of the other party. Therefore, such an intention is not to be presumed in interpreting a statute, unless there is unmistakable evidence that a breach of treaty obligations was intended by the legislator.[20]

[18] Case *Fürst G. und Genossen v. H.*; decision of June 27, 1909, RGZ 71, 293, 295-296.

[19] Decision of June 2, 1881; RGStr. 4, 271.

[20] Case of *H. und Th. und Genossen v. E.*; RGZ 24, 12, 13.

Despite the fact that article 4 of the bankruptcy law annulled conflicting state laws, the treaty was applied.[21]

From the cases discussed in the preceding pages, it must be concluded that the *Reichsgericht* took the view that treaties could, as regards their character as German laws, be abrogated by a subsequent federal statute; they were, however, in all cases interpreted with the presumption that no violation of treaty obligations had been intended by the legislature. No case could be found in which a German court refused to apply an internationally valid treaty, because it conflicted with a subsequent German law.

The practice of the courts of the Empire was, therefore, in entire harmony with the " dualist " theory on the relation between international law and municipal law. The influence of the theories of Triepel, Laband and Gneist is especially evident in the famous decision of the *Reichsgericht* on Oct. 26, 1914, known as the *Patentcase*. This was a suit by a German against a non-resident Frenchman and involved the patent rights of the latter under the Paris Convention for the Protection of Industrial Property of 1883. It was argued that the treaty had been terminated by the World War and that therefore Frenchmen could not claim its benefits. The court, however, said:

Even if it be admitted that the binding force of the convention under international law ceases *ipso facto* towards those states with whom we are at war, with the outbreak of the war, this does not annul that part of the convention which has become incorporated into our municipal law. . . . *The international and the internal validity of a treaty are not necessarily interdependent.* The two stand and fall together only in the case of those treaties, the application of which would be inconsistent with the purpose of the conduct of the war. This, however, at least

[21] See also RGStr. 12, 381; RGStr. 19, 274-275; RGStr. 29, 391, 397-398.

from the point of view of German law, is out of the question in the case of a treaty which, like the convention of 1883, concerns merely matters of private law. German international law [22] is far from sharing the view of certain systems of foreign law, that war must be conducted so as to cause as much economic damage as possible to the nationals of the enemy states and that, therefore, such nationals are to be deprived, to a large extent, of the benefits of common civil law. On the contrary, the principle applies that the war is conducted only against the enemy state and against its armed forces, and that nationals of enemy states enjoy equality with German nationals with regard to civil law, to the same extent as before the war in all respects, except in so far as statutory exceptions exist.[23]

The court here took the view that a treaty might be terminated as between the contracting states, and yet remain in force in its character as a municipal law. It is not indicated whether this refers only to treaties terminated by war, or whether the court intends to say that a treaty which is terminated between two states by mutual agreement would still continue in force as a municipal law. This has never been maintained by any German court.

The court seems to rest its decision on the argument that the international validity of treaties and their obligatory force in German law are not necessarily interdependent, and that the treaty was, therefore, not *eo ipso* terminated in German municipal law when it ceased to be binding on Germany in international law. However its statements on the principles of " German international law " give the impression

---

[22] This is a most unfortunate expression; the court evidently wishes to say that Germany recognizes as a rule of international law the principle that war is waged between states only, and not against the private citizens of the adverse party—a principle which had, before the World War, been generally accepted in Continental Europe, but which was not recognized by England and America. On this point, see *infra*, pp. 151-152.

[23] Case *H. H. v. L. Ch. in Paris*; RGZ 85, 375, 376 (italics inserted). See *supra*, p. 29.

that, in the opinion of the court, Germany recognizes as a rule of international law the principle that the nationals of the adverse party, who are not enrolled in the armed forces of the enemy, shall not be deprived of the benefits of common civil law, such as was embodied in the convention of 1883. This would indicate that Germany did not consider the treaty abrogated by the outbreak of war as between the contracting states.

It is unfortunate that the court has not expressed itself more clearly as to when treaties remain obligatory in German municipal law after having been terminated in their character as international contracts. The question has recently again been discussed by the *Reichsgericht* [24] without, however, throwing more light on the question. The *Patentcase* is of interest, nevertheless, as an example of the influence which the " dualists " had on German judges.

In conclusion it may be said that the courts of the Empire enforced treaties which had received legislative approval and which had been published in the *Reichsgesetzblatt*. Such treaties were regarded as having the character of federal statutes. In a conflict between a treaty and a later statute, the courts interpreted the latter with the presumption that the legislator had not intended to violate the earlier treaty.

[24] See *infra*, pp. 71-75.

CHAPTER III

Customary International Law 1871-1919

RULES of customary international law have frequently been applied by the courts of the Empire. The following cases may be cited:

In the case *Ziemer v. Rumänien,* the Prussian *Kompetenz-gerichtshof* [1] said of the rule of customary international law that one state is immune from the jurisdiction of the courts of another state:

The rule of international law, recognized by all the other great civilized states, that the property of foreign states may not be attached, is operative on Prussian courts, although this rule is not expressed in any Prussian statute or in any treaty concluded by Prussia.[2]

To the argument that this rule of customary international law conflicted with article 24 of the code of civil procedure, the court replied: " The legislature of the German Reich did not and could not intend any violation of generally recognized rules of international law, when enacting article 24 of the code of civil procedure." [3]

The *Kompetenzgerichtshof* again applied this rule of customary international law in the case of the Turkish war ships *Ismir* and *L'Assari Tewfik.* This was a case in which a creditor of the Turkish government, a German national,

---

[1] Court for the determination of jurisdictional conflicts between two courts or between a court and the administration, established by the law of April 8, 1847. Its seat is Berlin.

[2] [3] Decision of Jan. 14, 1882; ZPOR 16, 262.

asked for an attachment of two Turkish warships lying at Kiel, for payment of claims which had been allowed by a court in Constantinople. Both the lower court and the *Kompetenzgerichtshof* refused to attach the ships. The latter said:

The claim of the plaintiff is of a purely private law nature. The rule that such a claim may not be pleaded against a foreign state is not contained in the municipal law and particularly not in the statutes of the Empire. . . . The question whether a foreign state is subject to our jurisdiction is not to be decided by municipal law but solely by international law.[4]

In the case *Bardorf v. Belgien,* the *Reichsgericht* refused to take jurisdiction over a suit instituted by a German against Belgium. The court said:

The *Oberlandesgericht* [5] has very properly stated that this question [whether a foreign state may be made the defendant in a suit] cannot be decided in accordance with article 18 of the judiciary act, nor with article 232 of the code of civil procedure, but that, since no treaties dealing with this matter exist between Germany, Prussia and Belgium, and, there being no applicable provisions in the German statutes . . . the rules of international law must be applied.[6]

On Jan. 25, 1910, the *Kompetenzgerichtshof* rendered its decision in the well-known case *v. Hellfeld v. Russland.* The facts of this case were briefly the following:

In the course of transactions of v. Hellfeld with the Russian ministry of war during the Russo-Japanese war, Russia brought suit against v. Hellfeld. The latter brought in a counter-claim which was allowed substantially by the German

---

[4] Case of *Schönemann v. Ottomanischen Reichsfiskus*; ZPOR 13, 397; decision of June 14, 1902.

[5] Highest state court.

[6] Decision of Dec. 12, 1905; RGZ 62, 165.

consular court in Kiao-chow Sept. 27, 1909,[7] although Russia claimed that the court had no jurisdiction over the counter-claim. V. Hellfeld then brought action in the *Amtsgericht*[8] Berlin to have the judgment of the Kiao-chow court executed by an attachment of funds, belonging to the Russian government and deposited in a German bank in Berlin. At this point, the Prussian minister of foreign affairs raised the question of jurisdictional conflict, on the ground that the court had no jurisdiction to attach property of a foreign government, because a rule of customary international law exempted the latter from the jurisdiction of German courts. The case was thereupon brought before the *Kompetenzgerichtshof* which decided that the *Amtsgericht* was incompetent to issue an order of attachment against the property of Russia.

The contention of the minister of foreign affairs that there existed a rule of customary international law, according to which states were exempt from the jurisdiction of foreign courts, was challenged by v. Hellfeld. The latter sought to prove that courts in other states had taken a different view on this question and that writers on international law were not agreed whether such a rule existed. He stressed especially the point that no such rule had been recognized in Prussia and claimed that " there ought not to be a direct recourse to the law of nations, except in so far as there has been formed a German customary law ".[9] He argued furthermore that the German code of civil procedure did not permit suits to prevent the execution of valid judgments.

The *Kompetenzgerichtshof* refused to discuss the validity of the judgment of the Kiao-chow court, and stated that it was solely called upon to decide the question of the legality

---

[7] Cited in *American Journal of International Law*, vol. v, p. 496.

[8] Court of first instance.

[9] *American Journal of International Law*, vol. v, p. 500.

of the order of attachment. The parts of the judgment which bear on our inquiry are quoted:

The court said: "The decision . . . depends on whether in the case at bar the provisions of the code of civil procedure are to be applied, or whether other legal norms apply ".[10] It then stated that the case turned on the execution of a judicial decree and, consequently, on the exercise of judicial power. This judicial power of the state could not extend over another state, since states have equal rights and are independent of each other.

In so far as a state would not respect this relationship and would make arrangements to subject foreign states to the jurisdiction of its tribunals, such regulations would not be recognized by international law. *One must assume in interpreting and applying laws that the legislator has kept within the limits of the political power of the state. Hence, if the federal law contained no provisions affecting exterritoriality, the conclusion would be at once justified that the law does not refer to the subject and that rules of international law are of unconditional application.*[11]

The court then referred to articles 18-21 of the organic judiciary act which exempt foreign diplomats and their families and retinue from the jurisdiction of the German courts; it related that in 1884 a draft bill had been introduced in the *Reichstag* to supplement the judiciary act, in which it was declared that foreign states and their sovereigns were not subject to the jurisdiction of the German courts, and that the judiciary act intended to leave this rule of customary international law unaffected. This bill had been tabled, since it was considered impolitic to anticipate the further development of international law by a definite legal provision in Germany, and to bind Germany by a law, while

[10] *Ibid.*, p. 513.

[11] *Ibid.*, p. 513 (italics inserted).

other states were not so bound. The court pointed out that during the debates it was repeatedly stated that the legislature, in the enactment of the judiciary act, had in no wise intended to violate this rule of customary international law. The court said: " This basic principle [that no violation of international law was to be imputed to the judiciary act] and the additional point that the municipal law must be supplemented by the rules of international law were given general recognition during the debates of the *Reichstag*." [12] and later:

The interpretation which the judiciary act experienced at the hands of the legislature during these debates clearly indicates the legislative intent, and, therefore, furnishes an unequivocal basis for the direct application of customary international law to the question whether one state is subject to the judicial power of another. Viewed from this standpoint, the contention of the creditor [v. Hellfeld] that international law is applicable only insofar as it has been adopted by German customary law, lacks foundation in law. Such a legal maxim would, moreover, if generally applied, lead to the untenable result that in the intercourse of nations with one another, there would obtain not a uniform system—international law—but a series of more or less diverse municipal laws.[13]

In conclusion the court stated: " This decision is based directly on the principles of the law of nations ".[14]

In a decision of Jan. 3, 1884, the *Reichsgericht* was required to decide whether a brawl on a bridge between Prussia and Luxemburg had taken place in Prussia or in Luxemburg, i. e. the case depended on the delineation of the international boundary. The court said that " in the absence of written law, it is necessary to take into account what the theory of international law has established and what has

[12] *American Journal of International Law*, vol. v, p. 514.

[13] *American Journal of International Law*, vol. v, p. 514.

[14] *Ibid.*, p. 519.

become evident as legal maxims in the practice of the courts, and especially in treaties to which Prussia has been a party.[15]

The highest military tribunal, the *Oberste Militärgerichtshof,* had to decide whether rules of international law were applicable to the treatment of prisoners of war, in a case brought before it Feb. 9, 1916. Article 158 of the code of military justice stated that it should find " suitable " application to all criminal actions of prisoners of war. The code imposed a severe penalty on attempts at flight, but, according to article 8 of the Hague Convention on the Laws and Customs of War on Land of 1907, only a disciplinary penalty was to be imposed on prisoners who had made an attempt at flight. The court interpreted the term " suitable " in article 158 as follows:

The term " suitable application " means that the laws of war, recognized by Germany, must be taken into consideration. The legislator was aware of the special position which prisoners of war have under the law of nations. The " imprisonment of war " is a conception of international law which is determined today by the Hague Convention on the Laws and Customs of War on Land. Article 8, sections 2 and 3 contain the provisions for flight and attempts at flight.[16]

The court then stated that the Hague Convention had been signed and ratified by Germany, published in the *Reichsgesetzblatt,* and that subsequently there had been " no expression of the will of H. M. the Emperor to the contrary ".[17] It therefore imposed the disciplinary punishment only which

[15] RGStr. 9, 370; case of *v. W. und Genossen.* Rules of customary international law were furthermore applied in the following cases: Seuffert's *Archiv,* vol. 50, p. 97; RGStr. 2, 17, 18; RGStr. 32, 267; Goltdammer's *Archiv,* vol. xv, p. 77; *Entscheidungen der preussischen Obertribunale,* vol. 60, p. 18; RGStr. 3, 70.

[16] D. J. Z. (1916), p. 414.

[17][18] *Ibid.,* p. 414. See also decision of the same court in D. J. Z. (1916), p. 136.

is permitted by the Hague Convention, saying: " In so far and so long as the special position of prisoners of war is thus recognized by Germany, it must be taken into consideration by the judge as law of war ".[18]

This brief review of cases shows that generally recognized rules of customary international law, which had been accepted by Germany, were enforced by the courts.   It is not clear, however, whether the courts regarded such rules as having become transformed into German municipal law, in like manner as they regarded treaties to have become part of the municipal law.   On the contrary, some decisions seem to indicate a willingness on the part of some German judges, at least, to apply customary international law directly.   This is especially the case in the decision of the *Kompetenzgerichtshof* in *v. Hellfeld v. Russland*.[19]   The court there rejected the claim of the creditor " that international law is applicable only in so far as it has been adopted by German customary law ".   The following statements made by the court show, however, that it missed the point in question: The court argued that the acceptance of the maxim maintained by the creditor would lead to the result, that the intercourse of nations with one another would be regulated, not by a uniform international law, but by a series of diverse municipal laws.   In the case at bar the question was not one concerning international law as it regulates the relation between states, but rather that of international law as it is applied within one state by courts sitting under this state's jurisdiction.

The answer to the question whether customary international law was applied by the courts as international law proper or as part of German municipal law is to be found in a peculiar provision of the code of civil procedure which is, briefly, the following:

[19] See *supra*, p. 44.

A case may only be appealed to a higher court if the court of first instance has rendered a decision on a question of German federal law, or of German state law in force within two states or two Prussian provinces. Article 549 of the code of civil procedure states: " An appeal to a higher court must be founded on the argument that the decision of the lower court is based on the violation of a federal law, or of a law which is in force outside the district of the lower court's jurisdiction ". The term " outside the district of the lower court's jurisdiction " was interpreted in the sense that a law had to be in force in German territory at least the size of two states or two Prussian provinces, in order to fulfill the requirements of article 549 of the code of civil procedure.[20]

There existed thus two kinds of laws: one, called *Revisible Norm*,[21] giving the right of appeal to a higher court, the other, not *Revisible Norm,* being finally decided by the court of first instance.

Article 562 of the code of civil procedure states that the courts of appeal are bound by the lower courts' decisions on questions of such laws which are not *Revisible Norm*. It says: " The decision of the lower court on the existence and meaning of a law, the violation of which gives no right of appeal according to article 549, is binding on the court of appeal ".

Articles 549 and 562 of the code of civil procedure are not very clear. It was held in several decisions [22] that they must be interpreted in the sense that only *German* law, with the exception of local laws which are not in force in territory of the size of two states or two Prussian provinces, is *Revisible*

---

[20] See comments on articles 549 and 562 of the code of civil procedure, and cases cited in Sydow und Buch, *Zivilprozessordnung, Guttentag'sche Sammlung deutscher Reichsgesetze*, vol. xi.

[21] No short translation for this term could be found; it is therefore cited in German. It signifies a law which may be reviewed.

[22] RGZ 2, 13; RGZ 6, 412; RGZ 10, 115; RGZ 63, 318.

Norm and that foreign laws are not *Revisible Norm*. According to this interpretation of articles 549 and 562, the fact that a rule of law is *Revisible Norm* shows that this rule is not foreign, but German law. To illustrate the point:

If a case involving the interpretation of English law comes up in a German court, this court's interpretation of English law is final. The case may go to a higher court, if it also involves laws which are *Revisible Norm,* but the higher court must limit its review to such " reviewable " laws, and may not review the interpretation of English law by the lower court. The mere fact that the court of first instance has applied English law does not make this law, for purposes of appeal, a part of German law; the court has merely *referred* to the English law; it has remained a foreign law, however.

Suppose, on the other hand, that a case hinges on the question whether German *or* English law is to be applied, in other words, the first court has to interpret the rules of conflict of laws. In that case, the decision of the court of first instance on the rule of conflict of laws will be reviewed, because, as the *Reichsgericht* stated in its decision of July 5, 1915, the rules of conflict of law " are to be regarded as part of German law ".[23]

In a number of cases the *Reichsgericht* has declared that rules of customary international law are *Revisible Norm.* On June 16, 1883, this court held in the case *Preussischer Fiskus und Krone Preussen v. Fürstin v. Hanau:*

The European law of nations, created by the common consent of independent states, contains, both in so far as it is based on written law—international treaties—as on unwritten law—international custom—a number of legal rules whose interpretation may give rise to an appeal, notably so the laws of conquest in war.[24]

[23] Niemeyer's *Zeitschrift für Internationales Recht,* vol. 30, p. 264.

[24] J. W. (1883), p. 227; quoted from Triepel, *op. cit.,* p. 446; see also RGZ 14, 433; RGZ 16, 263; RGStr. 9, 370.

The decisions of courts of first instance on questions of customary international law have, as we have seen on the preceding pages, been reviewed by courts of appeal and by the *Reichsgericht*. In view of the fact that the courts are by law bound to reject appeals based on the interpretation of non-German laws by the courts of first instance, and that, on the other hand, the interpretation of rules of customary international law by courts of first instance has been the basis of appeals to higher courts, it must be concluded that the courts apply rules of international law as part of German municipal law. International law is not referred to, as is foreign law; it is applied as part of the municipal law of the land. It has been transformed into German law. In no other way could it have become *Revisible Norm*. To substantiate this conclusion, one more case may be cited:

In its decision of Feb. 25, 1904, the *Reichsgericht* rejected an appeal founded on the interpretation of the Convention of Bern on the Transport of Goods by Rail of 1890. The treaty had been signed and ratified, among others, by Austria and Germany. In this particular case, the treaty was applied as Austrian law, its violation having occurred in Austria and being, therefore, punishable in accordance with Austrian law. The court said:

The International Convention of Oct. 14, 1890 has created a uniform railroad transportation law in all the signatory states. This uniformity does not, however, amount to a formal unity of law, but is only a material similarity of law; it has been effected by each state's transforming the treaty into a law obligatory within its territory, *there being, on account of the sovereignty and independence of every state, no other way to create a uniform law in several states.* If this case were determined by German law, we should apply the Bern Convention— which has been ratified by Germany and published in the *Reichsgesetzblatt*—as *federal law,* and it could then come to this court on appeal and we should take jurisdiction; but in this case Austrian law has been applied which is not *Revisible Norm* according to articles 549 and 562 of the code of civil procedure.[25]

According to the court's statement there is no other way to create a uniform law in several states than by transformaion of a given law into the municipal law of every state. This general statement must be regarded as applicable to customary international law, as well as to treaties.

In conclusion it may be stated that the courts of the Empire applied generally recognized rules of customary international law, which they deemed to have been accepted by Germany, as part of German law. Conflicts between such rules and statutes were avoided by interpreting the latter with the presumption that no violation of international law had been intended by the legislator.

[25] *Kaiser-Ferdinand-Nordbahn v. M.*, RGZ 57, 142, 144 (italics inserted).

CHAPTER IV

ARTICLE 4 OF THE CONSTITUTION OF AUGUST 11, 1919

ARTICLE 4 of the constitution of the German Republic declares that: " The generally [*allgemein*] recognized rules of international law are deemed to form an integral and obligatory part of German federal law ".[1] The article has been widely discussed, both in Germany and elsewhere; opinions differ with regard to its exact meaning, as well as with regard to its intrinsic merits. It may therefore be of interest to briefly relate how this provision came to be included in the German constitution of 1919.[2]

The constitution of the German Republic was largely the work of Dr. Preuss. In his original draft, Preuss had put at the beginning of the constitution the following article (article 2):

[1] *Die allgemein anerkannten Regeln des Völkerrechts gelten als bindende Bestandteile des deutchen Reichsrechts.* The phrase " *allgemein anerkannte Regeln des Völkerrechts* " may be taken to denote rules of international law accepted by all states, or those accepted by only a majority. That the members of the national constituent assembly at Weimar intended it to refer to generally recognized rules of international law is clearly shown in the debates in the drafting committee. See *infra*, pp. 55-56.

[2] For further information on article 4 consult the following: Walz, " *Die Bedeutung des Artikel 4 der Weimarer Reichsverfassung für das nationale Rechtssystem* ", in Z. V., vol. xiii (1925), pp. 187 *et seq.*; Walz, *Die Abänderung völkerrechtsgemässen Landesrechts* (Berlin, 1927), pp. 93 *et seq.*; Wenzel, *Juristische Grundprobleme I: Der Begriff des Gesetzes* (Berlin, 1920), pp. 468 *et seq.*; Verdross, *Die Einheit des rechtlichen Weltbildes* (Tübingen, 1923), pp. 111 *et seq.*; Fleischmann, *Die Einwirkung auswärtiger Gewalten auf die deutsche Reichsverfassung* (Halle, 1925); Métall, " *Das allgemeine Völkerrecht und das innerstaatliche Verfassungsrecht* ", in Z. V., vol. xiv, pp. 161 *et seq.*

51

Sovereignty resides in the German people. In the affairs of the Reich it is exercised by the organs established by the constitution of the Reich; in the affairs of the states, by the German states in accordance with their state constitutions. The Reich recognizes the law of nations as an integral part of its own law.[8]

Dr. Preuss stated that this article contained the three fundamental principles of the new constitution, viz., first, the democratic principle, that sovereignty resides in the people, second, the federal principle, i. e. the preservation of the federal form of government for the new Republic, and third, the principle that the German Republic was a member of the society of states, and, therefore, accepted the law of nations.[4]

In the government draft, article 2 was divided into separate articles, which were inserted into the constitution in different places, so that the connection between them was destroyed. The third sentence of the article was changed to the form which it now has and included as article 3; it later became article 4. The original draft of Preuss accounts for the conspicuous position of the article at the beginning of the constitution, which has often been criticized; it has been maintained that the article ought to have stood in part VI which deals with the judiciary.

The article encountered considerable opposition in the committee of the national constituent assembly (*the Verfassunggebende Nationalversammlung*) which drafted the constitution. Representatives Kahl and Heintze objected that the world and particularly the Allied Powers would interpret it as a *captatio benevolentiae,* in view of the charges made against Germany during the war; they, furthermore, argued that the article would not effect any practical changes, as rules of international law had been

---

[8] Quoted from Métall, *op. cit.*, p. 164.

[4] Quoted from Verdross, *op. cit.*, p. 111.

applied by the *Reichsgericht* in many decisions.[5]   In defense of the article, Dr. Preuss drew attention to article 6, section 2 of the constitution of the United States, which causes treaties made under the authority of the United States to be the supreme law of the land.   He said: " Article 3 should have a similar but wider meaning ".[6]   Dr. Preuss frequently referred to Anglo-American jurisprudence and practice; he evidently wished to assimilate German jurisprudence and practice to that of England and America.   Article 3 was intended by him to make international law binding on German courts and citizens as the law of the land.

This desired result was frustrated through the introduction of a counter-proposal by representatives Haussmann and Quark, which stated that: " The relations of the German Reich with foreign states shall be regulated by treaties, the generally recognized rules of international law, and in the event that Germany enters the League of Nations, the rules set up by the League ".[7]   This self-evident and useless provision was unanimously accepted.   Thereupon Verdross published an article in defense of the government proposal,[8] in which he pointed out that the " Haussmann proposal " divested article 3 of all legal significance and did not accomplish the aim of Dr. Preuss, viz. to render international law obligatory on agents and citizens of Germany. The minister of justice, Dr. von Simson, also came to the defense of the government draft whose meaning he explained with the following words:

Article 3 desires to express the maxim dominant in Anglo-

---

[5] *Bericht und Protokoll des 8. Ausschusses über den Entwurf einer Verfassung des Deutschen Reiches* (hereafter cited as *Ber. u. Prot.*) 3. *Sitzung*, p. 31.

[6] *Ibid.*, 3. *Sitzung*, p. 32.

[7] *Ibid.*, 4. *Sitzung*, p. 33.

[8] D. J. Z. (1919), p. 291.

American jurisprudence and state practice that generally recognized rules of international law are binding not only on the state, but on individuals as well. It will not effect any material change in the practice of the German courts. The *Reichsgericht* has held, in many decisions, that international law fills gaps in the national legal system, and that rules of international law which by custom have been received into German law, and thereby have become German law, must be applied by the judges. In the proposed draft international law is recognized as a source of German law, with the restriction that this refers to " *allgemein anerkannte* " [9] rules of international law only. Anglo-American jurisprudence, too, does not interpret this principle in the sense that international law supersedes municipal law. It is rather maintained that the judge must apply municipal law if there is a clear conflict between municipal law and international law, while it is the duty of the state to abolish conflicts between its laws and the law of nations. Article 3 is important in cases where German federal law does not contain any rules pertaining to international law matters, or where the rules are not clear. In case of doubt, German municipal law must be construed in such a way that a conflict with international law is avoided. Article 3 is valuable as a rule of construction. The inclusion of this provision in the constitution is desirable, because it represents an acknowledgement of the value and validity of international law, and because it renders it difficult for our enemies to make the incorrect statement that international law is less respected in Germany than in England and America.[10]

Representative Haussmann now withdrew his counter-proposal stating that, before reading the article by Verdross, he had not been aware of the fact that his proposal would only bind Germany externally, i. e. in relation to other states; he said that since he " desired that international law should be binding both externally and internally " he would no

---

[9] See *supra*, p. 51, note 1.

[10] *Ber. u. Prot.*, 36. *Sitzung*, p. 406.

longer oppose the government draft.[11]   The latter was finally adopted as article 4.

Much discussion has centered around the question what was to be understood by " *allgemein anerkannte Regeln des Völkerrechts* ".   At the first reading of the draft in committee, Dr. Kahl objected that " nobody can answer the question what are recognized rules of international law "; [12] he feared that the article would subject Germany to rules which only a few states regarded as rules of international law, and which Germany had not accepted.   Preuss replied that for this very reason the word *allgemein* had been inserted; this had been done at the instance of the department of justice which had expressed similar apprehensions.   The department had declared that if this word was inserted, its apprehensions would cease, as it was thereby made impossible that " what England and America wish to be accepted as international law will be obligatory on us against our will ".[13] Preuss admitted that it was not always possible to state with precision what were " *allgemein anerkannte* " rules of international law.   In his view, however, rules which had not been accepted by all great powers could not be regarded as " *allgemein anerkannt* ".[14]   Dr. David stated that Germany could recognize as " *allgemein anerkannte* " rules of international law only those which it has accepted.[15]

At the second reading, Dr. Kahl declared that it was unanimously agreed that an " *allgemein anerkannte* " rule of international law in the sense of article 4 " was only such a rule as had been recognized by Germany ".[16]   This was also the

[11] *Ber. u. Prot.*, 36. *Sitzung*, p. 14.

[12] *Ber. u. Prot.*, 3. *Sitzung*, p. 6.

[13] *Ber. u. Prot.*, 3. *Sitzung*, p. 7.

[14] *Ibid.*, 3. *Sitzung*, p. 8.

[15] *Ibid.*, 3. *Sitzung*, p. 9.

[16] *Ibid.*, 36. *Sitzung*, p. 12.

opinion of Dr. Zweigert, the representative of the department of justice, who said that " it is self-evident that a rule of international law which conflicts with a prescription of German municipal law is no " *allgemein anerkannte* " rule." [17] Dr. David's statement: " The rules of international law which Germany has not accepted . . . are not " *allgemein anerkannt* "; the rules, however, which it has accepted are regarded by Germany as ' *allgemein anerkannt* ' ",[18] sums up the general view.

It is clear that the framers of the constitution did not limit article 4 to " universally " recognized rules of international law, but intended it to refer to " generally " recognized rules, which had to be accepted by Germany. Just how many other states must have recognized a rule, before it is " generally recognized " within the meaning of article 4 has, as yet, never been stated authoritatively. It remains for the German courts to give a definite meaning to the term.

It is certain, however, that a rule must have been recognized by Germany to be " generally recognized " within the meaning of article 4. The *Reichsfinanzhof* [19] stated in the *Goldtax case:* " The court can, therefore, not agree with the plaintiff's citation of article 4 of the constitution because, within its meaning, a generally recognized rule of international law must be one that has been recognized by Germany ".[20]

Another question which has received different answers is whether article 4 includes treaties? Anschütz, Stier-Somlo

[17] *Ibid.*, 36. *Sitzung*, p. 13.

[18] *Ibid.*, 3. *Sitzung*, p. 9.

[19] Federal court dealing with tax cases.

[20] Decision of Oct. 19, 1921; RFE 7, 102. See also Anschütz, *Die Verfassung des Deutschen Reiches* (Berlin, 1926), p. 62; Giese, *Die Verfassung des Deutschen Reiches* (Berlin, 1921), pp. 57-58; Stier-Somlo, *Deutsches Reichs- und Landesstaatsrecht* (Berlin, 1924), vol. i, p. 340.

and J. Schmitt [21] claim that treaties are comprehended in article 4, for the reason that one of the generally recognized principles of international law is the maxim *pacta sunt servanda*. As article 4 is intended to make generally recognized rules of international law binding on German courts and citizens as part of federal law, they argue, that via this maxim treaties are made immediately obligatory within Germany, as soon as they have become binding between Germany and the other contracting states.

This interpretation of article 4 does not take into consideration the fact that the maxim *pacta sunt servanda* addresses itself to states and requires them to observe their treaty obligations. It regulates the conduct of states as entities in relation to each other, and cannot be transformed into municipal law. So held by the *Reichsgericht* in a recent case:

A German pacifist had published an article in " *Das Andere Deutschland* ", a magazine, freely distributed in France, in which the German minister of war was accused of having violated the disarmament provisions of the Treaty of Versailles by enlisting volunteers (*Zeitfreiwillige*) during the civil disturbances of 1923 and 1924. The author was prosecuted for high treason under article 92 of the code of criminal procedure. The defense argued that because the maxim *pacta sunt servanda* had, through article 4, become part of German federal law, a citizen could not be prosecuted for high treason if, in compliance with this maxim, he publicly denounced Germany for having violated a treaty. The court rejected this contention, saying:

We must reject the proposition that the condemnation of a person for having publicly denounced violations of the Treaty

---

[21] Anschütz, *op. cit.*, p. 49; Stier-Somlo, *op. cit.*, p. 343; J. Schmitt, " *Konkordate, Völkerrecht und Artikel 4 der neuen Reichsverfassung* ", in *Zeitschrift für badische Verwaltung und Verwaltungsrechtspflege* (1921), pp. 199-202.

of Versailles constitutes a severe infraction of the generally recognized rule of international law: *pacta sunt servanda*. This maxim binds only the states who have concluded the treaty, and not individual citizens.[22]

The court found that there existed no rule of international law permitting citizens to inform another state of facts detrimental to the interest of their own country, and that, therefore article 4 did not apply.[23]

Although it cannot be argued on the basis of *pacta sunt servanda* that treaties are included in article 4, it may be said that German writers usually give the name " international law " to customary and conventional international law. The courts have, however, through their practice, implied that they do not regard treaties as included in article 4. If the latter were the case, it would become unnecessary to require that treaties be published before they become binding on courts and citizens. The courts have held otherwise.

In a case in which certain rights were claimed under a treaty between Germany and Poland which had not been published (treaty of Jan. 9, 1920), the *Reichsgericht* said: " We agree with the lower court's contention that the ratification of a treaty does not in itself affect the private rights of the plaintiff ".[24] And in its decision of June 18, 1927, the same court said, with regard to the treaty with Poland of May 15, 1922 which had been published:

The right of the plaintiff to deduce rights from the provisions of article 18 [of the treaty] has wrongly been denied by the defendant. The Geneva Convention is in fact a treaty between the two states [Poland and Germany], but it has been published

---

[22] *v. K. u. S.* Decision of March 14, 1928; RGStr. 62, 65.

[23] The court held that the minister of war had not violated the Treaty of Versailles, and that, therefore, the statements in the article were false.

[24] *C. v. Preussischen Staat*; Decision of June 22, 1922; RGZ 105, 156, 159.

in the form of a law (*Reichsgesetzblatt* 1922, ii. p. 253) and has therefore obtained force of law in Germany.[25]

As will be seen in the next chapter, the courts never refer to article 4 when applying treaties; they always require that a treaty be published, before they regard it as part of German law.

Article 4, therefore, refers to generally recognized rules of customary international law and declares that they must be deemed to form a part of German federal law. It is, as the majority of German writers say, a " general and permanent transformer " of generally recognized rules of customary international law, which are, by the article, adopted into German municipal law and rendered obligatory on courts and citizens.[26]

As we have seen in the preceding chapter, German courts had, previous to the constitution of 1919, frequently applied generally recognized rules of customary international law. Dr. Preuss and Dr. von Simson stressed the fact that the article would not materially change the practice of the courts; Dr. von Simson admitted that the " *Reichsgericht* has held, in many decisions, that international law fills gaps in the national legal system, and *that rules of international law which by custom have been received into German law, and thereby have become German law, must be applied by the judges.*" [27] Article 4 is, therefore, only declaratory of an established practice of the German courts. Why then the frequent references to Anglo-American jurisprudence, especially by Dr. Preuss?

[25] *G. v. Deutsche Reichsbahngesellschaft*; RGZ 117, 280, 284.

[26] Arndt, *Reichsverfassung* (Berlin, 1927), p. 62; Anschütz, *op. cit.*, pp. 46-47; Giese, *op. cit.*, p. 58; Hatschek, *Institutionen des deutschen Staatsrechts* (Berlin, 1923), vol. i, pp. 13-14; Walz, *Die Abänderung völkerrechtsgemässen Landesrechts* (Berlin, 1927), pp. 95-96; see especially the bibliographical references given there.

[27] *Ber. u. Prot.*, 36. *Sitzung*, p. 406 (italics inserted).

It seems that Dr. Preuss, and apparently also Dr. von Simson wished to assimilate German *doctrine* to Anglo-American doctrine, and felt that article 4 would bring the two legal doctrines closer.   As Dr. von Simson said: "Article 3 [4] desires to express the maxim dominant in Anglo-American jurisprudence and state practice that generally recognized rules of international law are binding not only on the state, but on individuals as well ".[28]   The classical German conception of international law as a *jus inter gentes* was to be abandoned.   That political reasons were largely responsible for the inclusion of the article in the constitution of the Republic is evident in the debates in committee.   Dr. von Simson urged that the article be accepted "because it makes it difficult for our enemies to make the incorrect statement that international law is less respected in Germany than in England and America ".[29]   Representative Haussmann exclaimed: " But international law, the treaties, and the League must be mentioned in the constitution! " [30]   Dr. Preuss desired an acknowledgment of the binding force of international law in the constitution, to demonstrate that the young German Republic respected international law, and referred as an example to the constitution of the United States (article 6, section 2).[31]   Dr. Delbrück describes the intentions of the framers of article 4 best when he says: "Article 3 [4] expresses a mental attitude rather than a legal norm ".[32]   It has, as a matter of fact, been regarded by some writers as a *captatio benevolentiae* and an implied admission that international law had not been respected in the German Empire in

[28] *Ber. u. Prot.*, 36. *Sitzung*, p. 406.

[29] *Ber. u. Prot.*, 36. *Sitzung*, p. 406.

[30] *Ibid.*, 3. *Sitzung*, p. 32.

[31] *Ibid.*, 3. *Sitzung*, p. 32.

[32] *Ber. u. Prot.*, 3. *Sitzung*, p. 31.

the same manner as in England and America.[33]   Even the repeated statements made in committee, that the article would not materially change the practice of the courts, can not obliterate the impression that the men who accepted article 4 believed that it would in some way assimilate German to Anglo-American jurisprudence.   On reading the minutes of the drafting committee one cannot help feeling that these men were not thoroughly familiar with the antithesis between international law and municipal law, and that they labored under a totally unwarranted conviction that Anglo-American doctrine differed materially from German doctrine, as regards the nature and binding force of international law.

Without wishing to go deeply into a discussion of the Anglo-American view on the relation between international law and municipal law, and the obligatory force of the former in municipal courts, we may say that the modern point of view in England and America is expressed in the following statement made by Willoughby:

It is true that these [English and American courts] adopt and apply established principles of international law, but in so applying and enforcing them they consider them as having been first impliedly adopted by the English or American state, as the case may be, as a portion of its municipal law.   Thus, in fact, these principles are received and enforced, not as international law, but as municipal laws.[34]

[33] See e. g. Oppenheimer, *The constitution of the German Republic* (London, 1923), p. 14 where he says: "Half a confession and half a protest, and withal a promise of better things for the future, it was obviously inspired by the well-known charges formulated during the war and in the Treaty of Versailles"; see also Freytag-Loringhoven, *Weimarer Verfassung in Lehre und Wirklichkeit* (München, 1924), pp. 390 *et seq.* Fleischman, *op. cit.*, pp. 22-23, complains bitterly that the article is based on a misunderstanding of modern Anglo-American jurisprudence, and an only too evident desire to "show ourselves as progressive, as only Anglo-Saxons can be".

[34] Willoughby, "Legal Nature of International Law", in *American*

This view on the relation of international law to municipal law does not differ materially from Triepel's doctrine.

As a matter of fact, article 4 has not brought any change in German *doctrine*. As stated before, the majority of writers regard it as a " general and permanent transformer " of international law, a conception based on the " dualist " theory of the antithesis between international law and municipal law.[35]

A very interesting interpretation of article 4 is to be found in Walz, *Abänderung völkerrechtsgemässen Landesrechts,*[36] and Schmitt, *Konkordate, Völkerrecht und Artikel 4 der neuen Reichsverfassung.*[37]   Both writers claim that, in addition to its function as a transformer of generally recognized rules of customary international law, by which the latter are made obligatory on citizens and courts, the article, furthermore, addresses itself to the legislature with the generally

Journal of International Law, vol. ii, p. 357. Compare also Oppenheim, *International Law* (London, 1928), p. 31 ; Picciotto, *The relation of international law to the law of England and of the United States* (London, 1915), pp. 104-105; Goodnow, *Comparative administrative law* (New York and London, 1902), p. 16.

[35] Verdross and Kunz have made the attempt to use article 4 as proof of their monistic theory of the supremacy of international law. They overlooked, however, that it is article 4, a municipal law, which requires German courts to enforce international law, and not international law itself. (Verdross, " *Staatliches Recht und Völkerrecht* ", in *Schweizer Juristenzeitung,* vol. xvii, p. 246; Kunz in *Annalen des Deutschen Reichs für Gesetzgebung, Verwaltung und Volkswirtschaft* (1921-1922), nos. 3 and 4, p. 295). In a later work, *Die Einheit des rechtlichen Weltbildes* (Tübingen, 1923), p. 115, Verdross appears to admit that article 4 is no proof for the correctness of the monistic theory, and that it is merely a " transformer " of rules of international law, through which these become obligatory on courts and citizens. The monistic theories of the Viennese School were rejected by the *Reichsfinanzhof* in the *Rhineland Ordinances* case, RFE 21, 68; see *infra,* pp. 82-83.

[36] Pp. 144-151.

[37] *Zeitschrift für badische Verwaltung und Verwaltungsrechtspflege* (1921), pp. 199-202 (1922), pp. 1-3.

recognized maxim of international law: *jus gentium consue-tudinarium et pactitium generale est praestandum.* In other words, a generally recognized rule of customary international law says that a state may not unilaterally modify the law of nations; a municipal law which conflicted with a generally recognized rule of international law is, therefore, from the point of view of international law, not legal, not law at all. By enacting such an illegal law, the legislature would violate the above mentioned maxim of international law which the constitution has declared to be part of German federal law. The law would, therefore, violate article 4; it would, conse-quently, be unconstitutional. In order for such a law to be binding on the courts, it would have to be enacted in accord-ance with article 76 of the constitution which requires a two-thirds majority for laws which modify the constitution.

The argument is an ingenious one and, if accepted by the courts, would make it difficult for the legislature to pass a law conflicting with a generally recognized rule of customary in-ternational law which had previously been recognized by Germany. Walz claims that since customary international law quite generally states that a state may not unilaterally modify international law, this refers also to treaty obliga-tions. In other words, article 4 serves to bind the legis-lature to abide by the rules of customary and conventional international law which it has once accepted, or, if it desires to pass a law violating these rules, the legislature must pass it in conformity with article 76 of the constitution.[38]

[38] The case differs from that obtaining in the United States where the constitution declares treaties and federal laws to be the supreme law of the land. Here both are deemed to be on an equal plane, because the constitution makes them both equally the supreme law of the land. Article 4, by declaring the generally recognized rules of customary inter-national law to be part of the law of the land, transforms also the very fundamental rule of international law, that it cannot legally be overruled by a municipal law, into German federal law. If this general rule is superseded by a statute which conflicts with a generally recognized rule

It may be doubted whether the framers of the constitution intended article 4 to have such far-reaching results. In speaking of Anglo-American jurisprudence, Dr. von Simson stressed the fact that there it is not maintained that international law supersedes municipal law, but that it is held " that the judge must apply municipal law if there is a clear conflict between [municipal law] and international law, while it is the duty of the state to abolish conflicts between its laws and the law of nations ".[39]   Dr. von Simson stated that this would also obtain in Germany, and regarded article 4 primarily as a rule of construction; he said: " In case of doubt, German municipal law must be construed in such a way that a conflict with international law is avoided ".[40]

The German courts have as yet not discussed this possible interpretation of article 4.   We have seen that the courts of the Empire never admitted that a German statute was intended to violate customary or conventional international law, although they declared that in case of a clear conflict, they would have to apply the statute.   In the cases decided since 1919, the courts of the Republic also never found that a clear conflict existed between German law and international law.   This will be seen in the following pages. The courts, therefore, have as yet not had occasion to discuss the interpretation of article 4, suggested by Walz and Schmitt.

of customary international law, or with a treaty, the general rule is no longer part of German federal law, therefore article 4 is violated, therefore the statute is unconstitutional.

As the German courts have, since 1919, asserted their right to review the constitutionality of laws and decrees (see RGZ 102, 161; RGZ 107, 315; RGZ 107, 370; D. J. Z. (1925), p. 1805; D. J. Z. (1926), p. 903; see also Mattern, *The Constitutional Jurisprudence of the German Republic* (Baltimore, 1928), pp. 590-609), such statutes would be declared unconstitutional by the courts.

[39] *Ber. u. Prot.*, 36. *Sitzung*, p. 406.

[40] *Ibid.*, p. 406.

The *Reichsfinanzhof,* however, in its decision of April 4, 1920, made the following significant statement: " A federal statute, which conflicts with an earlier international treaty which had [through publication] obtained the force of a federal law, would supersede this treaty, unless it excluded the cases regulated by the treaty." [41]   The court found no conflict between treaty and law in this case, but the above statement suggests that in case of a clear conflict the court would have applied the statute.

One must wait to see what the attitude of the courts will be towards the Walz and Schmitt theory.   At present, it seems unlikely that the courts will give such a far-reaching meaning to article 4.

[41] RFE 3, 10. See *infra,* p. 70.

CHAPTER V

Treaties Since 1919

According to article 45 of the constitution of 1919, the president concludes treaties, but " alliances and such treaties with foreign states as refer to matters of federal legislation require the consent of the *Reichstag* ".[1] The article closely resembles article 11 of the constitution of 1871. It was, however, stated in the committee of the national constituent assembly charged with drafting a constitution, by Dr. Preuss, representing the government, and reporter Ablass [2] that the consent of the *Reichstag*, required for the treaties enumerated in section 3 of article 45 is a *condicio juris* for the international validity of the treaty, i. e. that this consent must be obtained, before the treaty can be ratified. As seen in the chapter dealing with treaties in the courts of the Empire, this had been the practice of the government since 1871; today the necessity for this action is recognized by most German writers.[3]

In order to be enforceable in the courts, treaties must still be published in the *Reichsgesetzblatt*.[4] In the preceding chapter two cases were cited in which the courts held that a treaty had to be published to be binding on the courts.[5]

[1] Section 3, article 45.

[2] *Ber. u. Prot.*, pp. 282-283.

[3] See Anschütz, *op. cit.*, p. 163; Giese, *op. cit.*, p. 142; Wenzel, *Juristische Grundprobleme* (Berlin, 1920), pp. 489 *et seq.*; Hatscheck, *Deutsches und preussisches Staatsrecht* (Berlin, 1922), vol. ii, p. 485; Stier-Somlo, *op. cit.*, vol. i, p. 611.

[4] Arndt, *Die Verfassung des Deutschen Reiches* (Berlin, 1927), p. 709.

[5] See *supra*, pp. 58-59; the cases were RGZ 105, 156, 159; and RGZ 117, 280, 284. See also case of *v. Sch.*, decision of May 12, 1922; RGStr. 57, 61, 62.

The same was held by the *Reichsgericht* in its decision of June 12, 1923, where it was said of the Treaty of Versailles that " it has, upon its publication in the *Reichsgesetzblatt,* become a German federal law which, therefore, binds persons residing within Germany ".[6] And in a previous decision the same court had said: " The Treaty of Versailles has been published as a law and, and therefore, binds the judge ".[7]

The Treaty of Versailles was signed June 28, 1919 and came into effect Jan. 10, 1920. Its provisions were formally enacted into German law by publication of the treaty in the *Reichsgesetzblatt,* Aug. 12, 1919, and by the law of July 16, 1919 by which the assembly at Weimar approved of the treaty. In some cases the courts referred to the law of July 16, 1919, when enforcing provisions of the treaty.

The *Reichsfinanzhof* said in its decision of Oct. 15, 1920 that: " The Treaty of Peace of Versailles is not only an agreement between states which binds only the governments of the contracting powers, but it has been published as a German federal law and overrules, therefore, earlier federal tax laws which conflict with its provisions ".[8]

In *Deutsches Reich v. Sch.* the *Reichsgericht* held that the Treaty of Versailles overruled the German nationality law of July 22, 1913. According to the treaty, German nationals domiciled in the territory ceded to Poland acquired Polish nationality automatically as of Jan. 10, 1920; they could divest themselves of their new nationality by opting German, but until they so opted they were Polish. The court said:

Section 25 of the German nationality law of July 22, 1913, which stipulates that a German citizen . . . loses his German citizenship only if he has voluntarily acquired the nationality of a foreign state, is not applicable in this case, because the Treaty

---

[6] *B. und Söhne v. Dresdner Bank*; RGZ 107, 44, 47.

[7] *P. v. Stadt F*; RGZ 106, 56; decision of Dec. 11, 1922.

[8] RFE 4, 194, 196.

of Versailles, which has, by virtue of the law of July 16, 1919, become part of German federal law, overrules the earlier nationality law.[8a]

On March 14, 1928, the *Reichsgericht* said of the same treaty:

The Treaty of Versailles, which has become a German federal law by virtue of the law of July 16, 1919, and which has also been published as a German law, supersedes the provisions of the constitution, according to article 178, section 2 of the constitution, in such a manner that rules of German constitutional law which conflict with the Treaty of Versailles are suspended as long as the treaty remains in force.[9]

In *Firma B.K. & Co. v. Deutsches Reich* suit was brought against the German government for damages sustained by the plaintiff in making deliveries in kind to Yugoslavia, on account of reparations. *Inter alia,* plaintiff argued that the German ordinance of Oct. 29, 1923, by which deliveries in kind on account of reparations were declared suspended, had been annulled by the Agreement of London of Aug. 16, 1924. The court held:

Plaintiff claims that the ordinance of Oct. 29, 1923 was annulled by the final protocol of the conference of London of Aug. 16, 1924. The lower court rejected this proposition on the ground that the agreement was binding in international law only and could not modify or terminate a municipal law, such as the ordinance in question. The lower court has, however, overlooked the fact that the agreement . . . has obtained force of law internally by virtue of the law of Aug. 30, 1924. The agreement has thereby been transformed into German municipal law.[10]

[8a] Decision of Nov. 30, 1923; RGZ 107, 297, 299.

[9] RGStr. 62, 65; *v. K und S.*

[10] Decision of Nov. 29, 1927; RGZ 119, 156; see also *W. v. I. & Gen.*; decision of Apr. 9, 1920; RGZ 98, 257; and decision of May 17, 1927, cited in *Zeitschrift für ausländisches öffentliches Recht und Völkerrecht* (1929), vol. ii, p. 190.

Treaties which have been published in the *Reichsgesetz-blatt* will be enforced by the courts, provided they are self-executing.

In the case *F. v. Deutsches Reich,* the *Reichsgericht* rejected a claim based on article 74, section 2, and article 297 of the Treaty of Versailles, which state that the Reich shall indemnify its nationals for property lost by reason of the treaty. The court said:

The plaintiff has no direct claim against the Reich on the basis of article 74, section 2, and article 297 of the Treaty of Versailles. The Treaty of Versailles is an international treaty and therefore, on principle, binding only on the contracting states. It has, however, obtained force of law internally by virtue of the federal law of July 16, 1919. But individuals can derive rights from its provisions only in so far as they are clearly defined in the treaty, i. e. as the *Reichsgericht* has stated in some decisions (RGZ 117, 284; RGZ 119, 157, 162) when the provision in question is, by its content, purpose and form, capable of having effects in private law, without there being a necessity of further acts of an international law or constitutional law nature.[11]

The court held that article 74, section 2, and article 297 of the Treaty of Versailles were not self-executing:

The provisions of article 74, section 2, and article 297 have no such direct private law effects. They contain only the very general agreement between the Allies and Germany that the latter shall indemnify its nationals. In what manner Germany fulfills this treaty obligation was evidently of no interest to the Allied Powers. . . . From what has been said, it is clear that the provisions in question contain a rule obtaining between states only, and cannot give German nationals the right to prefer a claim against the Reich.[12]

[11] Decision of March 29, 1928; RGZ 121, 7, 9.

[12] RGZ 121, 7, 9, 10; in the same sense see RGZ 98, 257; RGZ 117, 284; RGZ 119, 157; compare also the decision of Oct. 8, 1895, RGZ 36, 183; *supra,* pp. 30-32.

Unless, therefore, the provisions of a treaty are self-executing, it is necessary to pass a law to carry them into effect. Thus the law of Aug. 31, 1919 was passed to execute article 309, section 1 of the Treaty of Versailles. The *Reichsgericht* applied this law and not article 309, section 1 of the treaty to the case *W. v. I. & Genossen,* decided April 9, 1920.[13]

As in the Empire, the courts admit that in a clear conflict between treaty and subsequent law, they will be bound by the later law. So held by the *Reichsfinanzhof* in a case decided April 4, 1920. The court had to decide whether the word " war contribution " which occurred in the treaty between Prussia and the Argentine of Sept. 19, 1827, referred to the special war assessment of 1918. The treaty provided that nationals of both countries should be free from war contributions, and the law of 1918 subjected *all* foreigners to the special war tax. The court decided that the tax was not a war contribution within the meaning of the treaty. Nevertheless, although no conflict existed the court said:

The treaty would . . . only·be binding on the German courts . . . if it had to be considered as a German law. The assent of *Bundesrat* and *Reichstag,* necessary for such a law, according to article 11, section 3 of the old constitution, has not been obtained. The question whether it must nevertheless be regarded in international law as a treaty of the Reich, and whether at the same time it must be considered to be a federal law, need not be decided; for *even if this were the case, the later statute . . . would prevail.*[14]

On Nov. 23, 1928, the *Reichsgericht* said with respect to

[13] RGZ 98, 257.

[14] RFE 3, 10; see also *supra,* p. 65 (italics inserted). The court here seems to maintain that a treaty concluded before 1870 by one of the German member states could not be enforced, because it had not received the approval of the *Reichstag* and *Bundesrat*. This view is not correct. See *supra,* pp. 32-37.

the German opium law of Dec. 30, 1920 which had been passed to carry into effect the provisions of the International Opium Convention of Jan. 23, 1912:

In interpreting the law, the International Opium Convention must be taken into consideration. It is, of course, conceivable that the opium law has not fully carried out the provisions of the opium treaty. In this case, the judge would, of course, be bound by the restrictions of the law. In case of doubt, however, it may be presumed that the legislator did not intend the law to fall short of the requirements of the treaty.[15]

The cases cited show that the courts of the Republic enforce treaties in much the same manner as those of the Empire. The international validity of treaties is distinguished from their obligatory force in German law and it is, on principle, admitted that in a clear conflict between a treaty and a subsequent statute, the court would be bound by the statute, but the latter will be interpreted with the presumption that no violation of treaty obligations has been intended by the legislator.

In the chapter dealing with the position of treaties in the courts of the Empire, a case was cited in which the *Reichsgericht* held that "international and internal validity of treaties do not necessarily depend on one another," and that a treaty, suspended or terminated by the outbreak of war, might, if its execution was not incompatible with the conduct of the war, still remain obligatory as a municipal law.[16]

On May 23, 1925, the *Reichsgericht* rendered a decision in a case involving the same question. The facts of this case were the following:

In November 1919 the defendant acquired from the plaintiff certain immovable property which was duly entered in

[15] *G. v. N.* RGStr. 62, 369, 373. The court found that, in fact, the law had gone further than the treaty.

[16] RGZ 85, 375; *supra*, pp. 37-39.

the land registry in Hamburg. The plaintiff subsequently asked that the entry be deleted as the defendant was a Russian subject, and as, according to the laws of Hamburg, the consent of the Senate of Hamburg was necessary for the acquisition of immovable property by aliens. The operation of the Hamburg law in question had been suspended by virtue of provisions of the Russo-German treaties of 1894 and 1904, which stipulated that the subjects of one contracting party may freely acquire immovable property in the territory of the other. Since the treaties had been published, they had superseded the Hamburg law.

The *Reichsgericht* held that the treaties of 1894 and 1904, being treaties of commerce, had been abrogated by the outbreak of the world war. The court did not discuss the question whether these treaties had not, despite the fact that they had been terminated between Russia and Germany through the outbreak of war, remained obligatory as German municipal laws. It declared that treaties of commerce are abrogated by the outbreak of a war, apparently both internationally and internally.

Defendant argued that the Treaty of Brest-Litovsk of March 3, 1918 had re-enacted the substance of the treaties of 1894 and 1904, with respect to the right of Russian nationals freely to acquire immovable property in Germany, and that this treaty superseded the Hamburg law; it was claimed that the treaty of Brest-Litovsk had never been terminated as regards its character as a German law, which it had acquired after publication in the *Reichsgesetzblatt*.

The *Reichsgericht* agreed with the lower court that the Treaty of Brest-Litovsk had become a federal law by reason of its publication on June 7, 1918, and that it, therefore, superseded the Hamburg law. It also agreed with the lower court that the Treaty of Brest-Litovsk had never been expressly abrogated by either Russia or Germany internationally or in domestic legislation. Germany had, however, severed diplomatic relations with Russia Nov. 5, 1918, thus interrupting the execution of the treaty. The Russian government had declared a few weeks later in a radio manifesto " to all " that it regarded the treaty as terminated. Against this radio manifesto the German government did not protest, and, furthermore, by evacuating the Russian territory which it had occupied in accordance with the treaty, Germany had tacitly accepted Russia's declaration. The *Reichsgericht* thus found that in the fall of 1918 there actually existed no treaty between Russia and Germany.

The lower court had concluded that since the Treaty of Brest-Litovsk, though tacitly abrogated in international law, had not been terminated internally by the German government, it continued in force as a municipal law. The *Reichsgericht* decided otherwise.

Taking into consideration the historical events of the fall of 1918, the Armistice Agreement by which Germany agreed to terminate the Treaty of Brest-Litovsk, the treaty of Rapallo of 1922, in which the Brest-Litovsk treaty was not mentioned, and the memorandum accompanying the draft of a law for the execution of the Treaty of Rapallo, in which it was stated that Germany and Russia had had no treaty relations since the fall of 1918, it came to the conclusion that:

It was not and did not appear necessary to the German governmen to issue (apart from the legal steps taken after the defeat of Germany in the World War for the execution of the Treaty of Versailles) any special proclamation addressed to German nationals, expressly abrogating the Treaty of Brest-Litovsk which everybody knew to have lost its object by the force of circumstances. *With regard to such after effects of a lost war, formalities normally requisite for the abrogation of international agreements cannot be required.* Admitting in other cases the propriety of a distinction with regard to the question how far the rights of individuals, resulting from an international treaty, are affected by events which interrupt peaceful relations between nations—for instance, in the case of treaties of commerce or industrial property conventions—such a distinction between its force in international law and its force in municipal law is impossible in the case of a treaty like that of Brest-Litovsk, *the political, military, economic and private law contents of which form an indivisible whole. Here each part depends upon the whole, stands or falls with it, both as to external and as to internal validity.*[17]

The *Reichsgericht* did not overrule its previous decision in which the Convention of Paris of 1883 was held to have continued in force as a municipal law, although suspended or terminated between Germany and France by the outbreak of the World War.[18]   The court re-affirmed the principle stated in the earlier case, viz. that treaties might continue in force internally, after having been terminated by force of circumstances between the contracting states.   But it denied that the Treaty of Brest-Litovsk " the political, military, economic and private law contents of which form an indivisible whole " had remained obligatory as a municipal law, after having been terminated as between Germany and Russia.

The position taken by the *Reichsgericht* in these two cases is that treaties of a purely private-law nature remain obligatory as municipal laws, unless their execution is incompatible with the conduct of the war, but that treaties whose execution cannot be reconciled with the aims of warfare, and treaties whose political, economic, military and private law contents form an indivisible whole, are simultaneously terminated as international contracts and as internal laws.

[17] *S. E. v. G. & G.*; RGZ 111, 40, 44-45 (italics inserted).   The treaty of Brest-Litovsk, having been held to have ceased being obligatory as a municipal law before the time of the relevant entry in the land registry, and the entry, having been effected without the permission of the Senate of Hamburg, it was declared to be invalid.

[18] RGZ 85, 375, 376; see *supra*, pp. 37-39.

The tendency of the *Reichsgericht* is apparently to limit the number of treaties which remain internally effective after having been terminated as international contracts. It excludes treaties of commerce and ranges them with political treaties and treaties incompatible with the conduct of the war. The two decisions have left the status of treaties, which are terminated between the contracting states by force of circumstances, in an unsettled position. The reasoning of the court in the Brest-Litovsk case is not clear, and the argument that, as regards the after effects of a lost war, " formalities normally requisite for the abrogation of international agreements cannot be required " [19] is not convincing. It is not clear whether the court rests its decision on the exceptional circumstances of the case—implying thereby that ordinarily the treaty would have had to be expressly terminated internally by an act of the government—or whether it states as a principle that treaties such as that of Brest-Litovsk are always terminated simultaneously, as between the contracting states, and in regard to their legal force in municipal law.

It is to be hoped that the *Reichsgericht* will soon take occasion to clarify its position with regard to the internal effectiveness of treaties which have been terminated by war, or under circumstances such as those which terminated the Brest-Litovsk treaty.

In conclusion it may be said that the position of treaties in German courts has not changed since 1919. The courts are still in entire harmony with the " dualist " theory and apply treaties as part of German federal law. The courts never mention article 4 when applying treaties; they evidently do not regard treaties as having been included in the term " generally recognized rules of international law ", as used in article 4.

[19] RGZ III, 40, 45.

CHAPTER VI

Customary International Law Since 1919

In several cases the courts applied rules of customary international law without mentioning article 4.

The *Kompetenzgerichtshof* decided a case, on Nov. 13, 1920, which arose out of the delivery of 2000 papercloth suits by the plaintiff to the Turkish ministry of war in 1918. Plaintiff sought to have certain accounts of the Turkish government in Berlin banks attached to secure payment for his claim. The court said: " In the case at bar we have to apply the generally recognized rule of international law that a state is usually not subject to the jurisdiction of another state ".[1]

In a case dealing with the extradition of a criminal from Czechoslovakia, the *Reichsgericht* applied the rule of customary international law that a person may be prosecuted only for the crime for which he has been extradited. The court said: " Since there are no treaty regulations on this subject, we must apply the rules of customary international law ".[2]

In its decision of March 10, 1928, the *Kompetenzgerichtshof* again refused to entertain a suit against a foreign state— in this case Poland—because, " according to an established rule of international law, a foreign state is not subject to the jurisdiction of the courts ".[3]

---

[1] J. W., vol. 50, p. 1478. The court continued to say that a state may voluntarily submit itself to the jurisdiction of another state, and found that Turkey had done so in this case, by depositing money with German banks as security for the payment of the goods delivered by plaintiff.

[2] Decision of April 4, 1921; RGStr. 55, 284, 285. *v. M.*

[3] *Halig v. Polen*; Z. V., vol. xv, p. 271. Compare also decision of the same court of March 12, 1921; J. W., vol. 50, p. 1481.

In a number of cases the courts applied rules of customary international law, stating that these had, by virtue of article 4, become part of German federal law.

The *Kompetenzgerichtshof* refused to entertain a suit against Poland for damages incurred by the plaintiff during the revolution; the court said that according to customary international law German courts had no jurisdiction over foreign states, and " by virtue of article 4 of the constitution, this generally recognized rule of international law must be deemed to form an integral part of German law ".[4]

The same rule of customary international law was applied by the *Reichsgericht* in the case of the ship " *Jonas Sill.*" This was a suit instituted by the German owner of the ship " *Jones Sill* " against the owners of the ship " *Ice King* " for damages sustained in a collision. The " *Ice King* " was a United States Shipping Board vessel. The U. S. Shipping Board protested, stating that the ship was the property of the United States, and that the court had consequently no jurisdiction.

The *Reichsgericht* agreed with the lower court that, in spite of some decisions of foreign courts, the rule of customary international law that states enjoy immunity in foreign courts, even for acts committed in the course of a commercial enterprise, had found general recognition before the war and had consistently been adhered to in German courts. It then proceeded to examine whether this rule had undergone any change during or after the war. After a careful review of the opinions of writers, international conventions and the Hague rules of the International Law Association of Sept. 3, 1921, the court concluded that:

Although there exists evidently a general desire to limit the immunity granted to foreign states, nevertheless this develop-

[4] Decision of Dec. 4, 1920; J. W., vol. 50, p. 1485.

ment [in literature] has not penetrated into the practice of international trade in a manner that would justify the conclusion that the above rule of international law has undergone a recognized change (see also article 4 of the constitution of Aug. 11, 1919).[5]

In a case involving the principle that extradited criminals may be prosecuted only for the crime for which they have been extradited, the *Reichsgericht* said:

It is true that German federal law does not contain such a rule of law; it must, however, be recognized as a rule of international law and applied in the case at bar, since there exists no treaty with Hungary which would otherwise govern the case. . . . This rule of international law, since it is generally recognized, constitutes an integral part of German federal law, according to article 4 of the constitution.[6]

The obligatory force of rules of customary international law in the German courts was more thoroughly discussed in a decision of the *Oberlandesgericht* of Darmstadt, December 20, 1926.

A prosecution arising out of alleged acts of tax evasion had been instituted against a member of the Chinese legation in Germany. It appeared that in consequence of certain irregularities said to have been committed by the defendant, in connection with his having divested himself of his previous German nationality, the German foreign office refused to recognize him as a member of a legation entitled to diplomatic privileges, and that it had informed the court accordingly. The diplomat pleaded immunity to the prosecution. The court said:

The question whether the accused enjoys extraterritoriality must

---

[5] *G. S. v. U. S. Shipping Board*; decision of Dec. 10, 1921; RGZ 103, 274, 276.

[6] Decision of March 18, 1926; RGStr. 60, 202. *v. Gr.-L.*

be answered solely according to municipal law. *Rules of international law are applicable only in so far as they have been recognized as municipal law, either by an express order, by customary law, or by conclusive act.*

According to article 18 of the judiciary act, the jurisdiction of the courts does not extend to diplomatic representatives and members of foreign legations, received by Germany. . . . These provisions do not state under what circumstances a person must be considered to be a member of an accredited mission. . . . The law must, therefore, be supplemented by such legal rules as may legitimately be applied. These rules are naturally to be found in the law of nations; and at this point article 4 must be taken into consideration, which declares that the generally recognized rules of international law are to be deemed to be part of German federal law.[7]

The court then found that diplomats enjoy extraterritoriality only when they have been accredited and that the accused had not been accredited.[8]

The court stated in this case that international law can be applied in German courts only when it has been received into German municipal law. This reception or transformation may, according to the court, take place by express order, by customary law or by conclusive act. Before 1919 rules of customary international law had become part of German law by customary law, since 1919 they are transformed by express order, viz. by article 4 of the constitution.

The case is based on the classical German doctrine of the separateness of the two legal systems, international law and municipal law.

The *Reichsfinanzhof* accorded immunity to a foreign diplomat in its decision of May 28, 1927 because of the same

---

[7] *Chinese Embassy case*; Z. V., vol. xiv, p. 594; J. W., vol. 56, p. 2324 (italics inserted).

[8] The court used the term "extraterritoriality", but actually referred to diplomatic immunity.

" generally recognized rule of international law " which, said the court, " constitutes an integral part of German federal law, according to article 4 of the constitution ".[9]

That rules of customary international law are applicable to certain relations between the German states was stated in the famous *Donauversickerungsfall*, decided by the *Staatsgerichtshof* [10] June 17-18, 1927. The facts of the case were:

The river Danube loses water subterraneously in its upper course. It was alleged by the German states of Württemberg and Prussia that this loss of water was caused by water works erected in the state of Baden on the Danube. They claimed that according to a rule of customary international law, co-riparians of international rivers are limited in the use of the water of such rivers, and may not by artificial means cause damage to the other riparian states. As regards the validity of rules of international law in controversies between German states, the court said: " In so far as the [German] states can act as independent states . . . their legal relations are governed by the law of nations, i. e. by the generally recognized rules of international law which, according to article 4 of the constitution, form part of German federal law.[11]

As is seen in the cases cited, the German courts sometimes mention article 4 and at other times fail to invoke it. This attitude shows that they do not consider article 4 as having changed the position of international law in the courts. The article, or perhaps more correctly, the general discussion of the antithesis between international law and municipal law

[9] *Zeitschrift für ausländisches öffentliches Recht und Völkerrecht* (1929), vol. ii, p. 202.

[10] A constitutional court, created by article 108 of the constitution; of 1919; see also articles 15, 18, 19, 59, 90, 170, 171 and 172 of the constitution.

[11] RGZ 116, annex p. 18; see also RGZ 112, annex pp. 21, 28 for decision of the *Staatsgerichtshof* in the case *Bremen v. Preussen*.

which it caused in German literature, have served to clarify the views of the courts on the relation between international law and German law; the article has established this relationship on the basis of Triepel's "dualist" theory. The acceptance of the latter by the courts is today no longer a matter of doubt.

The relation between international law and German law was most thoroughly discussed by the *Reichsfinanzhof* in the well-known *Rhineland Ordinances case*, decided Dec. 7, 1926.

The case concerned the validity of articles 7 and 8 of ordinance no. 1 of the Interallied Rhineland High Commission. According to Article 3 (a) of the Rhineland Agreement of June 28, 1919, the Interallied Rhineland High Commission was given "power to issue ordinances so far as may be necessary for securing the maintenance, safety and requirements of the Allied and Associated forces". It was provided that such ordinances, when duly published, should have the force of law, and should be recognized as such by all Allied and Associated military authorities and by the German civil authorities. Ordinance no. 1 of the Interallied Rhineland High Commission was passed under the power given by article 3 (a) of the Rhineland agreement of 1919. Articles 7 and 8 of the ordinance stated that the German laws and decrees, intended to operate in the occupied territories, should not come into force before having been submitted to the Interallied Rhineland High Commission. Germany protested that the ordinance exceeded the powers granted to the commission by article 3 (a) of the treaty of 1919, but the commissioner of the Reich submitted regularly for registration the laws and decrees relating to the occupied territories.

In the present case the appellant, the owner of a tile factory in the Cologne district, omitted to pay the coal tax for the period between Aug. 1, 1923 and Oct. 14, 1923, during which that district had been occupied by allied troops.   In July 1925 the appellant had been sued by the tax authorities for recovery of the coal tax alleged to be owing.   It was asserted on behalf of appellant that the German coal-tax law of March 26, 1923 had not been in force in the territory occupied by allied troops, because the law had not been registered with the Interallied Rhineland High Commission, and that the appellant was accordingly under no duty to pay.

The court proceeded to examine the validity of articles 7-8 of ordinance no. 1 of the Interallied Rhineland High Commission.   In this connection the court made the following significant statement:

International law creates rights and duties only between states (Triepel, *Völkerrecht und Landesrecht*, pp. 110, 287); it addresses itself exclusively to states and not to the agents of states (e. g. the judges) or to their citizens. *The latter are subject only to municipal law; to international law only in so far as it has by statute or by custom been transformed into municipal law.* All international treaties obtain force of law for courts and citizens only after their " transformation " or " reception " into municipal law (" *Transformationslehre* ", see Strupp, *Grundzüge des positiven Völkerrechts,* 3rd ed. 1926; p. 12).[12]

The court then rejected the argument made by counsel for the defense, that Triepel's theory had been superseded by a new theory, that of Kelsen and the Viennese School, which is based on the supremacy of international law.   It said:

This theory represents, as Strupp expresses it on p. 12, only an " opinion " (*Postulat*); it might perhaps lead to a supremacy of international law in the future. For the present, such a supremacy of international law cannot be recognized; on the contrary, for the present, this court adheres to the theory estab-

12 Z. V., vol. xiv, p. 440, 444; RFE 21, 68, 73 (italics inserted).

lished by Triepel (*Transformationstheorie*) and applies it to the ordinances of the Interallied Rhineland Commission.[13]

It was claimed by counsel for the defense that the *Transformationslehre* did not apply to the occupied territories because the ordinances of the Interallied Rhineland High Commission had obtained force of law for persons residing there, not by transformation into German municipal law, but by military force.   The court rejected this claim, saying:

The "*Transformationstheorie*" applies also to the occupied territories, and the ordinances of the Interallied Rhineland Commission are obligatory on the German judge only in so far as they are authorized by German municipal law.   The Treaty of Versailles and the Rhineland Agreement have been published in the *Reichsgesetzblatt*.   The provisions of these two international treaties have thus become part of German federal law; this is especially true of article 3 (a) of the Rhineland Agreement which grants to the Interallied Rhineland Commission a limited right to enact ordinances.   The ordinances of this commission have the force of German municipal law only by virtue of article 3 (a) of the Rhineland Agreement which has become a German federal law.[14]

The court then stated that according to German law courts may examine the validity of laws and ordinances and may declare them invalid if they violate a higher law.   The right of judicial review applied also to the ordinances of the Interallied Rhineland High Commission, there being no rule of international law opposed to it.

[13] Z. V., vol. xiv, p. 445; RFE 21, 74.   The court here rejected the theory of the "monists" that international law is *for a municipal court* superior to municipal law.   Triepel also maintains that international law is a law superior to municipal law, but only for the states which are bound by international law and not for private persons who are never bound by international law directly, and for whom only the municipal law of their country is obligatory.

[14] Z. V., vol. xiv, p. 446; RFE 21, 75.

The court then said that articles 7 and 8 of ordinance no. 1 would be valid only if they conformed to the higher law from which they derived their authority, viz. the Rhineland Agreement. It found that by requiring German laws and decrees to be registered with the Interallied Rhineland High Commission, the latter had exceeded its legislative powers under the Rhineland Agreement. The only right which could be deduced from article 3 (a) of that treaty was that the commission might forbid the putting into effect of such German laws as might threaten the security of the army of occupation, but not that German laws could be made dependent upon previous registration with the commission. The coal-tax law was, therefore, held to have been obligatory and the defendant condemned to pay the tax.

This decision is of importance because it establishes the basis on which German courts enforce customary and conventional international law. International law is enforced through German courts only after it has been transformed into German municipal law. The case firmly upholds Triepel's " dualist " theory; it also shows that article 4 has not brought any change in the application of international law by the courts of the Republic.

CHAPTER VII

Conclusions

TREATIES are applied by the courts after they have been published in the *Reichsgesetzblatt*. They are deemed to form part of German federal law and supersede earlier statutes. They may be superseded by a subsequent statute; however, in the absence of unmistakable proof to the contrary, statutes are construed with the presumption that they contain an implied reservation to the effect that they shall not be applied whenever their provisions conflict with obligations under a treaty which has been published in the *Reichsgesetzblatt*.

Treaties dealing exclusively with private law matters will probably continue to be enforced by the courts as part of German federal law, after they have been terminated or suspended between the contracting states by the outbreak of a war.

Rules of customary international law which are generally recognized and which have received the assent of Germany are applied by the courts. They are deemed to form part of German federal law. Statutes are construed with the presumption that they contain an implied reservation to the effect that they shall not be applied whenever their provisions conflict with generally recognized rules of customary international law which have received the assent of Germany.

Rules of customary and conventional law which have through transformation or adoption become part of German federal law supersede the laws of the German member states, because of the maxim " federal law supersedes state law ", expressed in articles 2, section 1 of the constitution of 1871 and article 13 of the constitution of 1919.

PART II

SWITZERLAND

CHAPTER I

Introduction

THE relation between international law and municipal law has not been systematically examined in Swiss literature. Fleiner's commentary on the Swiss constitution [1] contains a few remarks on the enforcement of treaties in Swiss courts. Burckhardt [2] discusses the effects of treaties in municipal law generally, but without specific reference to Switzerland. Both Burckhardt and Fleiner are " dualists ", but Burckhardt is not entirely in agreement with Laband. Burckhardt agrees with Laband that theoretically a distinction must be made between the international validity and the internal effectiveness of treaties, but claims that in practice no such distinction exists. In practice, he says, treaties become valid internationally and internally at the same time, because, unless the constitution of a state expressly declares the contrary, it is always to be presumed that treaties become internally binding upon exchange of ratifications and publication of the treaty. [3]

[1] Fleiner, *Schweizerisches Bundesstaatsrecht* (Tübingen, 1923), pp. 753 *et seq.*

[2] Burckhardt, "*Die staatsrechtliche Wirkung der Staatsverträge*", 34 *Zeitschrift für schweizerisches Recht* (neue Folge), pp. 145 *et seq.* See also Nippold, *Der völkerrechtliche Vertrag, seine Stellung im Rechtssystem* (Bern, 1894). Nippold distinguishes strictly between a treaty as an international contract and as a municipal law; see especially pp. 70, 95-96, 125-126, 139-142.

[3] *Ibid.*, pp. 146 *et seq.* The internal effect of treaties in Swiss municipal law is briefly discussed in Kundert, *Völkerrechtlicher Vertrag und Staatsvertragsgesetz im schweizerischen Recht* (Zürich, 1919). Kundert is in agreement with the classical German doctrine.

Before discussing the view taken by the Swiss courts towards international law, it is advisable to explain briefly the peculiar structure of the Swiss government.

Swiss constitutional law is based on the principle of the *confusion des pouvoirs,* the co-mingling of the powers of government. In this it distinguishes itself from the constitutional law of most modern democracies which have adopted the principle of the *separation des pouvoirs,* the separation of the powers of government. Article 60 of the Swiss constitution of 1848 states: " The supreme power of the Confederacy is exercised by the *Bundesversammlung* ".[4] This principle was reaffirmed in article 71 of the constitution of 1874.[5] However, a part of the judicial power of the Federation has been delegated by the constitution of 1874 to a federal court, the *Bundesgericht,*[6] which was made independent of the *Bundesversammlung.* In so far as the judicial power has been delegated to the *Bundesgericht,* it is withdrawn from the control of the *Bundesversammlung.*

While there is no separation of powers in Swiss constitutional law, it is possible to speak of a separation of functions: the *Bundesversammlung* fulfills primarily legislative, the

---

[4] " *Die oberste Gewalt des Bundes wird durch die Bundesversammlung ausgeübt* ". The *Bundesversammlung* is a popularly elected assembly of two houses; the *Nationalrat* represents the people; the *Ständerat* the several Swiss cantons.

[5] The constitution of May 29, 1874 is in force today; several amendments have been added since 1874, notably one (article 84) which subjects treaties concluded for more than fifteen years, or for an indeterminate duration, to a popular referendum, if demand is made by 30,000 Swiss citizens entitled to vote, or by 8 cantons.

[6] Article 106 of the constitution of 1874. The *Bundesgericht* consists of 24 members and 9 substitutes elected by the *Bundesversammlung* for six years. The court is divided into chambers; two chambers deal with civil cases, three with criminal cases in original jurisdiction, one with criminal cases on appeal from the highest cantonal courts, and one chamber acts as a constitutional court (*staatsrechtliche Abteilung*).

Bundesrat [7] executive and the *Bundesgericht* judicial functions. But this separation of functions is true to a certain extent only. In a number of matters, as, for instance, the conclusion of treaties, the executive power is exercised by the *Bundesversammlung,* and the *Bundesrat* merely carries out the decisions of the *Bundesversammlung.* Certain judicial powers are reserved to the *Bundesrat* and the *Bundesversammlung*: the *Bundesrat,* and, on appeal the *Bundesversammlung* decide cases of administrative law, so-called *Administrativstreitigkeiten,* [8] acting as a constitutional court (*Staatsgerichtshof*). The *Bundesversammlung* and the *Bundesrat* have, therefore, executive, legislative and judicial functions which are not always clearly delimited and which overlap frequently. The *Bundesgericht,* however, has judicial functions only.

[7] The *Bundesrat* consists of 7 members, elected by the *Bundesversammlung* for three years. Each member heads one of the administrative departments of the government, but their decisions are rendered collectively. One of the members is elected president of Switzerland for one year. The *Bundesrat* acts as a body always.

[8] Articles 189, 192 of the *Bundesgesetz über die Organisation der Bundesrechtspflege.*

CHAPTER II

TREATIES

THE fact that the Swiss constitution does not recognize the principle of the separation of powers has an important bearing on the position of treaties in Swiss municipal law.

Article 85 of the constitution [1] vests the treaty-making power in the *Bundesversammlung;* article 102 declares that the *Bundesrat* shall watch over the interests of the Confederacy in its international relations and shall deal with the foreign affairs of the state. Treaties are, therefore, concluded in the following manner: the *Bundesrat* carries on negotiations with the foreign state or states, and appoints representatives to sign the treaty. The *Bundesversammlung* then ratifies the treaty, and finally the *Bundesrat* exchanges ratifications and causes the treaty to be published. [2] The functions of the *Bundesrat* are ministerial, those of the *Bundesversammlung* executive. [3]

[1] When the term "constitution" is used, reference is made to the constitution of 1874, now in force.

[2] The formula employed by the *Bundesrat* when exchanging ratifications is as follows: "The *Bundesrat* of the Swiss Confederacy, having examined the treaty signed ... by the representatives of the Swiss *Bundesrat* and those of the government of ..., the treaty having been approved by the Swiss *Nationalrat* on ..., and by the Swiss *Ständerat* on ... [follows text of the treaty] declares the above treaty ratified and in its entire extent in force."

[3] In exceptional cases the *Bundesversammlung* has by law authorized the *Bundesrat* to conclude treaties without first obtaining its approval: e. g., the law on extradition of Jan. 22, 1892 authorized the *Bundesrat* to conclude reciprocity conventions with foreign states, without submitting them to the *Bundesversammlung*; the law on the organization

Swiss constitutional law differs from that of most modern democracies in that here the treaty-making and the law-making powers are vested in one organ, the *Bundesversammlung*. The *Bundesrat* is authorized to issue decrees to carry out the laws of the *Bundesversammlung,* but in the enactment of laws as well as in the conclusion of treaties the *Bundesversammlung* is the controlling organ. Fleiner draws the following conclusions therefrom:

The distinction between executive and legislature,[4] which is dominant in foreign doctrines relative to treaties, is inapplicable to Switzerland, because, according to our constitution (article 71), the *Bundesversammlung* is not only a legislative organ, but is in certain matters the only competent organ; consequently, Switzerland can be bound in international law only by its [the *Bundesversammlung's*] consent; in other words, a treaty negotiated by the *Bundesrat* with a foreign power is valid in international law only after it has been ratified by the *Bundesversammlung*.[5]

of the telephone and telegraph service of Dec. 16, 1907 (article 5) authorized the *Bundesrat* to conclude special conventions with neighboring states on the basis of the Telephone and Telegraph Convention of 1868 (see Fleiner, *op. cit.*, p. 754, note no. 13).

Unless authorized by law, the *Bundesrat* may not conclude treaties or exchange declarations having the character of treaties. On Oct. 6-15, 1875 the *Bundesrat* exchanged declarations with Italy concerning the support of indigent nationals. The *Bundesversammlung* instituted a commission which was charged with the examination of the legality of the action of the *Bundesrat*. On the basis of the report of the commission, the *Bundesversammlung* passed a resolution on July 5, 1876, in which it asked the *Bundesrat* not to exchange declarations having substantially the character of treaties, before the *Bundesversammlung* had given its approval to such declarations. (*Amtliche Sammlung der Bundesgesetze und Verordnungen der Schweizerischen Eidgenossenschaft, neue Folge* (hereafter cited *A. S., n. F.*), series ii, p. 382; *Postulate der eidgenössischen Räte und ähnliche vereinzelte Vorschriften, neue Folge,* p. 87).

[4] "*Regierung und Parlament*".

[5] Fleiner, *op. cit.*, p. 753.

In the case *Lepeschkin v. Obergericht Zürich,* the *Bundesgericht* stated that the ratification of a treaty by the *Bundesversammlung* constituted an executive *and* a legislative act:

The acceptance of a treaty by the *Bundesversammlung* has juridically a twofold significance: it signifies, on the one hand, ratification of the treaty, which makes the treaty binding on Switzerland in international law, and which authorizes the *Bundesrat* to exchange ratifications; and, on the other hand, it betokens the act which gives the treaty force of law and makes it obligatory on the agents of the state and on private persons.[6]

A statement to the same effect was made by the *Bundesrat* in answer to an inquiry by the Dutch legation as to whether treaties became, immediately upon ratification, binding on private persons in Switzerland. In September 1906 the Dutch legation received the following answer from the *Bundesrat*:

The *Bundesversammlung* approves all treaties with foreign powers, in accordance with article 85, section 5 of the constitution; the *Bundesrat* does not exchange ratifications—whereby Switzerland would be bound internationally—until the *Bundesversammlung* has ratified the treaty. . . . Since acceptance of the constitution of 1848 it has been held that treaties, even those modifying existing legislation, have force of law, without the necessity of passing a statute.[7]

Approval of a treaty by the *Bundesversammlung* renders the treaty simultaneously binding on Switzerland in international law and obligatory on courts and private persons in Swiss municipal law. According to the above statement of the *Bundesrat,* treaties overrule earlier statutes; they have,

---

[6] Decision of Feb. 2, 1923; BGE 49. i. 188, 195. Included in the term "agents of the state", are courts.

[7] Quoted from Burckhardt, *Schweizerisches Bundesrecht* (Frauenfeld, 1930), vol. ii, p. 520.

therefore, at least force equal to that of Swiss federal statutes.

In order to be binding on courts and private persons in Switzerland, laws must be published in the *Amtliche Sammlung der Bundesgesetze und Verordnungen der Schweizerischen Eidgenossenschaft,* an official collection of federal laws and decrees. The law of Oct. 9, 1902 prescribes that treaties also must, as soon as ratifications have been exchanged, be published in this official collection.[8] As to the significance of publication for the legal force of treaties within Switzerland, the *Bundesrat* made the following statement in its answer to the Dutch legation:

It is nowhere expressly stated whether treaties become obligatory on private persons and agents of the state only *after* they have been published. Treaties which impose obligations on the state as such and not on private persons are occasionally published after having come into force [internationally]. On the other hand, *treaties which impose obligations on private persons have always been published before coming into force [internationally].*[9]

The *Bundesgericht* has on one occasion only expressed its view with regard to the effect of publication on the enforceability of a treaty in Swiss municipal law. In this instance, the court had been asked by the *Bundesversammlung* to give an opinion on the following question: The Treaty of Algeciras, which Switzerland had not signed, created certain special courts for foreigners in Morocco. Article 45 of the treaty stipulated that a final appeal should lie from these courts to the Swiss *Bundesgericht.* The *Bundesversammlung* asked the *Bundesgericht* to state whether it could be given this jurisdiction by the Treaty of Algeciras. The

---

[8] *Ibid.,* p. 520.

[9] Quoted from Burckhardt, *op. cit.,* vol. ii, p. 520 (italics inserted).

court decided that it was necessary that Switzerland conclude a treaty with the signatories of the Treaty of Algeciras, expressing acceptance of article 45 of the latter, before it could take the jurisdiction provided in article 45. In the course of its opinion, the *Bundesgericht* made the following statement with regard to the international and the internal validity of treaties:

A treaty concluded by the constitutionally competent organs of the state binds the state internationally; the treaty becomes binding internally, i. e. it becomes obligatory on private persons and agents of the state, as soon as it has been published in due form; the treaty thereupon becomes a federal law. . . .[10]

The *Bundesgericht* held that treaties, like federal statutes, must be published in the official collection of federal laws and decrees before they can be enforced in the courts. In view of the fact that, whenever they impose obligations on private persons, treaties are published immediately after ratifications have been exchanged, there is no divergence between the time when a treaty becomes binding on Switzerland in international law and obligatory on courts and private persons in Swiss municipal law.[11]

[10] *Botschaft des Bundesrats* of March 5, 1907, in *Schweizerisches Bundesblatt,* 1907 (ii), pp. 112 *et seq.* On June 19, 1907, Switzerland exchanged declarations with the signatories of the Treaty of Algeciras, accepting the jurisdiction given to the *Bundesgericht* in article 45 of the Treaty (*A. S. n. F.,* vol. xxiii, pp. 310-312).

[11] Article 84 of the constitution which subjects federal laws to a popular referendum if, within 90 days after the approval of the law by the *Bundesversammlung,* request is made by 30,000 citizens entitled to vote, or 8 cantons, was amended on Jan. 30, 1921. Since 1921, all treaties concluded for more than 15 years or for an indeterminate duration are equally subject to a popular referendum if demand is made by 30,000 citizens or 8 cantons. Ratifications for such treaties are not exchanged until the 90-day period has elapsed within which a popular referendum may be requested. The 1921 law has further assimilated the procedure by which statutes and treaties attain force of law in Switzerland.

Despite the fact that in Switzerland international validity and internal effectiveness of treaties occur simultaneously —due to the concentration of treaty-making and law-making power in one organ, the *Bundesversammlung*—Swiss jurisprudence, nevertheless, distinguishes between a treaty as an international contract between states, and as a Swiss law. In the previously mentioned case *Lepeschkin v. Obergericht Zürich,* the *Bundesgericht* said in this connection:

The obligation of the judiciary to enforce the provisions of a treaty does not flow from the treaty itself which creates an obligation between the contracting states as subjects of international law only; in addition, an act of the constitutionally competent organ of the state is required which orders that the provisions of the treaty be executed, and by which they [the provisions of the treaty] are given force of law within the state.[12]

The court then cited with approval the theories of Laband and Fleiner.

A distinction between international validity and internal effectiveness of treaties was also drawn by the attorney-general in the case of *Ivan de Justh.* Ivan de Justh, a Hungarian national, had assaulted Count Bethlen, the Hungarian premier and delegate to the League, in Geneva.[13] The attorney-general argued that article 43 of the Swiss federal criminal code applied to the case. This article makes assaults on the representatives of foreign powers, accredited to Switzerland, punishable by fine and imprisonment. The argument of the attorney-general rested on the assertion that the scope of article 43 had been extended by article 7, section 4 of the League of Nations Covenant which had been ratified by Switzerland. According to the Covenant, the delegates to the League shall enjoy diplomatic immunities and privileges. The attorney-general stated:

[12] Decision of Feb. 2, 1923; BGE 49. i. 188, 196.
[13] June, 1926.

The question with which we are here confronted is whether article 43 has been extended through article 7, section 4 of the League of Nations Covenant, according to which the delegates to the League and the permanent officials of the League shall enjoy diplomatic privileges and immunities. The League of Nations Covenant has, upon its acceptance by the Swiss people [14] and publication in the Swiss official collection of laws, obtained the force of a municipal law in Switzerland.[14a]

The argument of the attorney-general was the following: Article 43 of the federal penal code punishes assaults against accredited diplomatic representatives in Switzerland. Since the League Covenant had the force of a federal law, it extended article 43 of the penal code to include the punishment of assaults against the delegates to the League. Therefore, he said, the article applied to the assault made by Ivan de Justh on Count Bethlen. He concluded: " The provisions of article 7, section 4 of the League of Nations Covenant have consequently force of law in Switzerland. Switzerland is obligated, both in international and in municipal law, to grant diplomatic privileges and immunities to the delegates to the League." [15]

The statements of writers and judges, quoted on the preceding pages, show that Swiss jurists adhere to the dualistic theory, i. e. that they distinguish between the obligatory force of treaties on private persons and courts in Swiss municipal law on the one hand, and on Switzerland in international law on the other hand; they admit that the former does

[14] The League of Nations Covenant was voted on by a popular referendum on May 16, 1920; see Fleiner, *op. cit.*, p. 314.

[14a] Quoted from Burckhardt, *op. cit.*, vol. iv, pp. 552-553.

[15] Quoted from Burckhardt, *op. cit.*, vol. iv, pp. 552-554. In the opinion of the attorney-general, inviolability constituted one of the privileges and immunities of diplomats. The *Bundesgericht* took jurisdiction of the case and punished Ivan de Justh in accordance with article 43 of the federal criminal code; decision of July 14, 1926; see *infra*, p. 108.

not *ipso jure* follow from the latter, but is conditioned on an act by the constitutionally competent organ which invests the treaty with the force of a municipal law.

The *Bundesgericht* has not hesitated to apply a treaty, even when it conflicted with an earlier federal statute. In *Schweizerische Kreditanstalt v. Schweizerischen Postfiskus* the court held that the treaty with Austria of 1868 overruled the provisions of the federal postal law of 1849. It said: " The postal treaty in question has, without doubt, force of law; its provisions have the character of municipal laws adopted by the Swiss legislative power on the basis of a contractual agreement [with Austria]." [16]

In *Müller & Cie. v. Nordostbahngesellschaft* the *Bundesgericht* said that " the contents of international treaties . . . which Switzerland has concluded, are a source of Swiss federal law within Switzerland." [17] The court did not intend to distinguish between a law and a source of law, but meant to say that the content of treaties is part of Swiss federal law.[18]

In their character as federal laws, treaties are on principle equal to federal statutes. In *Lepeschkin v. Obergericht Zürich* the *Bundesgericht* stated: " The provisions of treaties which have been approved [by the *Bundesversammlung*] have equal force with those of a municipal law, and must be enforced by the organs of the state, as long as they have not been duly abrogated. . . ." [19]

From this equality between treaties and federal laws Fleiner draws the conclusion that conflicts between a treaty and a law must be solved by application of the maxim *lex posterior derogat priori*. He says:

[16] Decision of Oct. 24, 1884; BGE 10, 583, 585.
[17] Decision of May 1, 1901; BGE 27. i. 192, 194.
[18] See Fleiner, *op. cit.*, p. 757.
[19] BGE 49. i. 188, 196.

The later treaty overrules previously enacted federal law, and the later law would overrule an earlier treaty. However, the latter case must not be assumed where there exists a doubt; that interpretation of the law must be sought which leaves the treaty law in force as a special law alongside the more recent statute.[20]

Fleiner's view is that treaties have no superiority over federal statutes, but that treaties must be regarded as special laws; in other words, that, unless a later federal statute is clearly intended to abrogate an earlier treaty, the maxim *lex posterior generalis non derogat legi priori* determines the relation of treaty and subsequent statute.

In a number of cases the *Bundesgericht* was called upon to decide whether a federal statute had abrogated an earlier treaty.[21] It has consistently expressed the view that no violation of treaty obligations had been intended by the *Bundesversammlung* and that, consequently, the treaty remained in force.

In the case of *Kiesow* it merely stated this view without giving any reasons for it. The court said:

> The above mentioned provision of the treaty of 1869 has by no means been abrogated *ipso jure* through the coming into force of the federal law of Dec. 17, 1879, as is maintained by appellee; on the contrary, it remained binding on both parties to the treaty until the latter was legally terminated between them.[22]

[20] Fleiner, *op. cit.*, p. 758.

[21] Case of *Kiesow*; BGE 7, 774; case of *Schweizerische Kreditanstalt v. Schweizerischen Postfiskus*; BGE 10,583; case of *Stübler*; BGE 18, 189; case of *Schmid*; BGE 18, 198; case of *Köster*; BGE 19, 122; case of *Forquet de Dorne*; BGE 19, 134; case of *Lux*; BGE 21, 76; case of *Zimmermann*; BGE 21, 57; case of *Attorre*; BGE 21, 342; case of *Bundesrat v. Kanton Bern*; BGE 22, 942; case of *Rieger*; BGE 22, 1025; case of *Canderan*; BGE 21, 705; case of *Hof v. Turuvani*; *Semaine Judiciaire* (1901), p. 118.

[22] Decision of Dec. 3, 1881; BGE 7, 774, 783; see also case of *Zimmermann*; BGE 21, 57; case of *Forquet de Dorne*; BGE 19, 134; case of *Attorre*; BGE 21, 342.

In *Schweizerische Kreditanstalt v. Schweizerischen Post-fiskus* the *Bundesgericht* rejected the claim of appellant that the federal laws of 1849 and 1876, relating to the postal service in Switzerland, applied to a claim for damages which arose in connection with a parcel post shipment from Austria to Switzerland. It held that the Postal Treaty of July 15, 1868 alone applied to this specific case " as it is self-evident that two different, possibly conflicting legal norms cannot apply to the same legal relationship and to the identical questions of law ".[23] It applied the treaty which in the court's opinion continued to govern shipments of parcel post from Switzerland to foreign countries and *vice versa*, even after the passage of the federal postal law of 1876.

In the case of *Stübler*, in which it was claimed that the extradition of Stübler was illegal, because it violated the federal extradition law of 1892, the court said:

It is true that, as a rule, persons are not extradited for crimes committed in the territory of the state which is asked to extradite them, and that this rule is expressly stated in article 12 of the federal extradition law of Jan. 22, 1892. However, the extradition law did not intend to overrule conflicting provisions of existing treaties, *nor could it do so without violating international obligations.*[24]

In the case of *Lux* the court said: " The case is solely governed by the treaty [of extradition of 1874] which could not be changed by the unilateral legislative act of one of the states parties to the treaty ".[25]

In the case of *Martin v. Renold* the same court declared that " as a matter of principle, a treaty *cannot* be changed by

---

[23] Decision of Oct. 24, 1884; BGE 10, 583, 585.

[24] Decision of June 17, 1892; BGE 18, 189, 193 (italics inserted).

[25] Decision of March 2, 1895; BGE 21, 76, 79.

a later federal law, *because it binds Switzerland in relation to the foreign* [contracting] *state* ".[26]

The language of the *Bundesgericht* in these cases, especially in *Martin v. Renold,* lacks precision and clarity; it is therefore possible to misinterpret them, and to claim that the court abandoned the " dualist " theory [27] and held that because treaties are superior to municipal statutes in the sphere of international law, it follows that they are also superior to Swiss statutes in a Swiss court, i. e. in the sphere of municipal law.[28]   On closer examination, however, it will be found that the court took a different line of reasoning.

The court's argument rests on the presumption that the *Bundesversammlung* does not intend to violate international law.   It is briefly this : Abrogation of a treaty by a municipal statute constitutes a violation of international law by the state which passes the statute; the *Bundesversammlung* does not desire to violate international law, *consequently no abrogation of the treaty has been intended by the passage of the statute.*

In our discussion of the position of treaties in German courts we found that statutes conflicting with earlier treaties were interpreted with the same presumption, viz. that the legislature did not intend to violate the international obligations of the state, contained in a treaty, by passing a statute.[29]

[26] Decision of Sept. 9, 1909; BGE 35. i. 594 (italics inserted).   In the same sense : case of *Attorre*; BGE 21, 342; case of *Canderan*; BGE 21, 705; case of *Rieger*; BGE 22, 1025.

[27] The *Bundesgericht* declared itself in accord with the " dualist " theory in *Lepeschkin v. Obergericht Zürich* (BGE 49. i. 188, 196; see *supra,* p. 97), where the question why municipal courts must enforce treaties was carefully examined.

[28] This is, however, the view taken by W. Kaufmann in *Die Rechtskraft des internationalen Rechts und das Verhältnis der Staatsgesetzgebung und der Staatsorgane zu demselben* (Stuttgart, 1899).   See *supra,* p. 14.

[29] See *supra,* p. 85.

This presumption is made practically irrebuttable in Switzerland. The *Bundesgericht* has never even considered the possibility that the *Bundesversammlung* might have intended to abrogate a treaty by passing a conflicting statute, despite the violation of the international obligations of Switzerland involved in such action.

The Swiss view is easily understood when we stop to consider that the Swiss legislature has both the treaty-making and the law-making powers. The *Bundesversammlung* can hardly be deemed desirous of violating an international obligation which it has itself incurred, and—what is even more important—which it can terminate in accordance with the rules of international law, whenever it so chooses.[30]

The *Bundesgericht* has never maintained that a treaty is not overruled by a subsequent Swiss statute, *because* the former is a law of superior force; in *Lepeschkin v. Obergericht Zürich* [31] the court expressly stated that the provisions of treaties have equal force with those of a municipal law. When it says that a later statute cannot overrule an earlier treaty, the court merely takes into consideration that, because of the peculiar structure of the Swiss government, an intention on the part of the *Bundesversammlung* to abrogate a treaty obligation by means of a federal statute cannot be presumed. The practice of the *Bundesgericht* in cases where Swiss statutes conflicted with earlier treaties is not due to a belief on the part of the court that, because treaties are, in their nature as international contracts between states, superior to the municipal laws of any one contracting state, such treaties must be enforced by a Swiss court regardless of subsequent conflicting statutes. In other words, the cases of conflicts between treaties and later laws do not indicate an

[30] The cases cited all dealt with treaties which could be terminated by giving notice to the other contracting party.

[31] BGE 49. i. 188, 196; see *supra*, p. 99.

abandonment of the " dualist " theory by the *Bundesgericht*. Fleiner's statement that such conflicts must be solved by applying the maxim *lex posterior generalis non derogat legi priori* accords with the practice of the *Bundesgericht*.[32]

Article 113 of the constitution declares that the *Bundesgericht*, as a constitutional court (*Staatsgerichtshof*), shall have jurisdiction over cases in which it is claimed that a treaty has been violated by a cantonal authority—executive, legislative or judicial.   This article makes it possible to carry a case from a cantonal court of first instance immediately to the *Bundesgericht*, whenever the cantonal court has refused to apply the treaty, or has misinterpreted it.   Violation of treaty obligations by executive acts of a canton, or by a cantonal law can be brought to the *Bundesgericht* which decides them in original jurisdiction.

Article 113 has been interpreted by the *Bundesgericht* to refer to treaties dealing with public law matters only.   In *Müller & Cie. v. Nordostbahngesellschaft* the court held that treaties dealing with private law matters were equivalent to federal private law and could be appealed to the *Bundesgericht* only after the highest cantonal court had rendered a decision in a case involving such treaties.[33]

Article 189 of the law on the organization of the judiciary

[32] The cantonal courts have followed the *Bundesgericht*; see case of *Andran et consorts v. Donque*; decision of the *Cour de justice civile* of Geneva, *Semaine Judiciaire* (1889), p. 423; case of *Les sociétés des auteurs, compositeurs et éditeurs de music à Paris v. V.*; decision of the *Tribunal de district* of Bern, *Droit d'Auteur* (1889), p. 99.

[33] BGE 27. i. 192, 194.   The court referred to article 182 of the law on the organization of the judiciary, which states that the jurisdiction of the *Bundesgericht* as a constitutional court is limited to federal public law; federal private law is enforced by the cantonal courts, subject to the final control of the *Bundesgericht*, but the latter takes jurisdiction only after the case has been decided by the highest cantonal court.   The view taken by the court that article 182 was applicable to treaties shows that the court regards them as federal laws, in no way superior to statutes.

declares that jurisdiction over "certain cases of an international law nature, i. e. those which arise in the application of treaties dealing with the following matters: commerce and customs, patent fees, freedom of trade, the rights of the nationals of the contracting parties to settle in their respective territories [*Niederlassung*], and exemption from the duty to furnish a substitute for military duty" is reserved to the *Bundesrat* and on appeal to the *Bundesversammlung*. Such cases are withdrawn from the jurisdiction of the cantonal courts and of the *Bundesgericht*.

The final control over the enforcement of treaties in Switzerland is exercised by the three organs of the federal government; treaties dealing with public law matters are immediately withdrawn from the cantonal courts to the *Bundesgericht*, and the enforcement of a great number of treaties is put into the hands of *Bundesrat* and *Bundesversammlung*. The Swiss constitution has taken care to insure the faithful execution of the treaty obligations of Switzerland.

The cases cited on the preceding pages enable us to define the position of treaties in the Swiss courts:

International validity and internal effectiveness of treaties coincide in Switzerland; treaties become obligatory on private persons and enforceable in the courts after exchange of ratifications and publication of the treaty in the official collection of laws.

Treaties overrule earlier federal statutes. When a federal statute conflicts with an earlier treaty, the courts interpret the former with the presumption that the legislature intended the treaty to remain in force as a special law alongside the more recent statute.

Treaties have force equal to *federal* statutes. Since federal law overrules cantonal law in Switzerland,[34] treaties overrule cantonal laws.

---

[34] *Übergangsbestimmungen zur Bundesverfassung*, article 2; see Fleiner, *op. cit.*, pp. 421, 758; see also BGE 7, 782; and BGE 24. i. 312, 318.

CHAPTER III

CUSTOMARY INTERNATIONAL LAW

IN the previous chapter it has been seen that the practice of Swiss courts in enforcing treaties is in accord with the "dualist" theory; in other words, that they take the view that, after publication in the official collection of laws, treaties are for Swiss courts equivalent to Swiss federal laws. The courts apply them as Swiss municipal laws.

It is not possible to define accurately on what basis Swiss courts enforce rules of customary international law. Such rules have frequently been applied by the courts,[1] but few cases indicate the reasons which prompted the courts to enforce customary international law. Under the circumstances we can do no more than state our opinion as regards the position of customary international law in Swiss courts, based on the few cases which appear to indicate the attitude of these courts. The available material is too meager to permit a dogmatic statement with regard to the position of customary international law in Swiss courts.

We shall first take into consideration article 112, section 2 of the constitution which authorizes the *Bundesgericht* to take original jurisdiction over "crimes and felonies against the law of nations."[2] The phraseology of this article is apt to be misleading; it may give the impression that the *Bundesgericht* is authorized to take jurisdiction over *all* vio-

---

[1] See cases cited *infra*, p. 110.

[2] "*Verbrechen und Vergehen gegen das Völkerrecht*".

lations of international law. Actually, the court has no authority to define crimes and felonies against the law of nations; it is merely given jurisdiction over cases governed by such federal statutes as have been enacted to make certain violations of international law a criminal offense in Swiss law. The statutes are the following:

Article 41 of the federal penal code declares that " any person who violates the territory of a foreign country or commits any other act against foreign states in violation of the law of nations ", is punishable by fine and imprisonment. The meaning of the article was explained by the federal department of justice[3] in an opinion submitted to the *Bundesrat* and the *Bundesversammlung* and accepted by them. The opinion stated that not all violations of the law of nations are by article 41 made a criminal offense in Swiss law. As the department said, " not in a single penal code are all violations of written and unwritten international law declared to be punishable ".[4] It was held that article 41 " is limited to acts endangering the peace of, and attacks against the existence or honor of a foreign state ".[4] Over such acts the *Bundesgericht* will take original jurisdiction.

Article 42 of the federal penal code makes punishable with fine and imprisonment " public insults against a foreign nation or its sovereign, or a foreign government ". Prosecution is instituted upon demand of the foreign government only, and on condition that the foreign government grant Switzerland reciprocity.[5]

---

[3] *Eidgenössisches Justiz- und Polizeidepartment.*

[4] Quoted from Burckhardt, *op. cit.*, vol. iv, pp. 548-550.

[5] On July 2, 1915 the *Bundesrat* enacted a decree by which insults against foreign states, their sovereigns or governments, as well as the sale or distribution of printed matter, pictures or other matters of a nature insulting to foreign states, was made punishable without the necessity of a demand by the offended government, and irrespective of whether that government granted Switzerland reciprocity. The decree

Article 43 of the federal code makes punishable with fine and imprisonment, " insults or assaults against the representatives of a foreign power which are accredited to Switzerland ".

There have been a few cases only in which the *Bundesgericht* took jurisdiction under article 112, section 2 of the constitution:

On April 16, 1879, Paul Brousse, the author of certain articles in the anarchist paper " *L'Avant-Garde* " was condemned to two months imprisonment and banishment from the country by the *Bundesgericht* for having committed " an act in violation of the law of nations by provoking and publicly agitating in favor of the assassination of kings and magistrates of foreign states (articles 41 and 42 federal penal code) ".[6]

On Jan. 27, 1916 the Swiss clerk Hunziker tore down the flag of the German consulate in Lausanne. He was condemned by the *Bundesgericht in contumacium* to one month imprisonment for " violation of the law of nations and article 41 of the federal penal code ".[7]

The most interesting case was that of *Ivan de Justh.*[8] De Justh was condemned by the *Bundesgericht* to the payment of a fine and banishment from the country for ten years; the court based its decision " on the verdict of the jury, applying articles 42 and 43 of the federal penal code ".[9] These two

was enacted to enable Switzerland to fulfill her neutral obligations; it was repealed Dec. 2, 1918 (see Burckhardt, *op. cit.*, vol. iv, pp. 527-528).

[6] *Bundesblatt der Schweizerischen Eidgenossenschaft* (1879), part ii, p. 548; (1880), part ii, p. 661; see also Salis, *Le droit fédéral suisse* (Bern, 1906), vol. iv, p. 691.

[7] Decision not published; see Burckhardt, *op. cit.*, vol. iv, p. 548.

[8] Quoted from Burckhardt, *op. cit.*, vol. iv, pp. 552-554; see *supra,* pp. 97-98.

[9] *Ibid.*, p. 552; decision of June 25, 1926; see also the case of *Schill,* cited in *Zeitschrift für schweizerisches Strafrecht*, vol. i, p. 316 and Cl. 1888, 638.

articles were held to apply to the assault made by de Justh on Count Bethlen, Hungarian premier and delegate to the League of Nations, by reason of article 7 of the Covenant of the League of Nations which had become part of Swiss law after its ratification by Switzerland and publication in the official collection of laws.[10]

Although the decisions in some of these cases are based on a " violation of the law of nations ", in addition to the violation of the Swiss federal penal code, the *Bundesgericht* did not actually enforce customary international law, but merely Swiss statutes which adopted certain rules of customary international law into Swiss municipal law, and made them a punishable offense in Swiss law.

The purpose of article 112, section 2 of the constitution is, probably, to place the enforcement of those federal penal statutes which aim to carry out within Switzerland certain international obligations of the state, in the hands of the *Bundesgericht* instead of the cantonal courts; the latter enforce all other federal statutes. Article 112, section 2 is a correlary to article 113, section 3 of the constitution, which places the enforcement of treaties of a public law nature—in so far as they have not been made subject to the jurisdiction of *Bundesrat* and *Bundesversammlung*—in the hands of the *Bundesgericht*.[11] The object of the two articles is evidently the desire to safeguard the enforcement of international law within Switzerland by withdrawing it from the jurisdiction of the cantonal courts, and placing it in the hands of the highest court of the country, the *Bundesgericht*.

In a number of cases the *Bundesgericht* and cantonal courts have applied rules of customary international law without, however, giving the reasons why these rules are obligatory on Swiss courts and on private persons. The

[10] *Supra*, p. 98.
[11] See *supra*, pp. 104-105.

Bundesgericht applied rules of customary international law in the following decisions: *Nägle* case [12] (rules of customary international law on extradition), *Lepeschkin v. Obergericht Zürich*; [13] *Hausner v. Banque internationale de commerce de Petrograd*,[14] *Schinz v. Obergericht Zürich* [15] (rules on recognition of states); *Erben Oswald v. Eidgenossenschaft* [16] (rules pertaining to international claims).

Rules of customary international law were applied by the *Bundesgericht,* acting in original jurisdiction as a constitutional court, in a number of cases between the several cantons. Thus in *Luzern v. Aargau* [17] the court interpreted the *clausula rebus sic stantibus* and decided the case by the application of rules of customary international law on the termination of treaties by one of the contracting parties; in *Ziegler Gebrüder v. Schaffhausen*,[18] and *Luzern v. Aargau* [19] the rules pertaining to international servitudes were applied; in *Schaffhausen v. Zürich* [20] those relating to sovereignty over rivers passing through different states, and in *Zürich v. Thurgau* [21] those relating to the obligations of states for the care of their indigent nationals abroad.[22]

[12] BGE 1, 411.

[13] BGE 49. i. 188.

[14] BGE 50. ii. 507.

[15] BGE 52. i. 218.

[16] BGE 52. ii. 235.

[17] BGE 8, 43.

[18] BGE 31. ii. 828; see also *American Journal of International Law,* vol. i, pp. 235 *et seq.*

[19] BGE 8, 43.

[20] BGE 23. ii. 1405.

[21] *Praxis des Bundesgerichts,* vol. iii (1914), p. 386.

[22] See also decision of the *Tribunal civil* of Geneva in the case *V. et Dicker v. D* (Cl. 1927, 1179). In discussing the immunity of diplomatic representatives, the court stated that this immunity was based "on the tacit agreement resulting from the fact that when a state admits a

The cases cited show that Swiss courts apply rules of customary international law when deciding cases calling for the application of the law of nations; they do not indicate on what ground the courts apply these rules. In *K. K. Österreichisches Finanzministerium v. Dreyfuss*,[23] however, the *Bundesgericht* made the significant statement that, in so far as international law is applied within Switzerland, it is to be regarded as Swiss law equal to federal law. There is no other case in which this or any other Swiss court has made a similar statement; it is, in fact, the only case in which the relation between international law and Swiss law is stated in clear terms. We shall, therefore, briefly state the facts of the case.

Dreyfuss, the owner of bonds issued by Austria through a bank in Switzerland, was entitled by lot to have his bonds redeemed in Swiss francs on July 1, 1916. He was denied payment by the *Basler Handelsbank,* because he refused to declare under oath that the bonds had been deposited in Switzerland before July 3, 1914, and that they did not belong to the subject of a state at war with Austria. This statement was required by an Austrian war decree, passed subsequent to the issue of the bonds. Dreyfuss applied for an order of attachment on the funds of the Austrian department of finance, deposited in the *Basler Handelsbank;* this was granted by the cantonal court of first instance.

The Austrian department of justice brought suit to set aside the order, asserting that the attachment was in reality levied against the Austrian state as *fisc,* and that, according to a recognized rule of customary international law, the funds

foreign diplomatic representative, it recognizes the right which custom, in other words, the law of nations, grants him ". The court evidently regarded this tacit agreement to deal with diplomatic representatives in accordance with international law as binding on it.

[23] Decision of March 13, 1918; BGE 44. i. 49.

of foreign governments were immune from attachment. The cantonal court of first instance, and the cantonal court of appeal held that this rule of customary international law did not apply when a state acted *jure gestionis*.[24]

The Austrian department of justice then carried the case to the *Bundesgericht*. With regard to the question of jurisdiction, the court said:

The argument that the attachment is invalid because of the rule of international law that foreign states enjoy immunity from the jurisdiction of our courts, raises a question of jurisdiction . . . and *the rule of international law* which determines it [the jurisdiction] *is to be regarded in Switzerland as Swiss federal law*, because, by its very nature, it lays claim to be generally in force within the state, *and has*, for this reason, *force equal to federal law*. The case, therefore, hinges on a question of jurisdiction determined by Swiss federal law. . . .[25]

The case seems to hold that the rule of customary international law which determines that a state shall not be subject to the jurisdiction of the courts of another state is one which by its very nature lays claim to be in force within states, and is therefore to be deemed part of the municipal law of states. The court does not make a general statement to the effect that *all* rules of customary international law must be regarded as Swiss federal law. It apparently draws the correct distinction between rules of customary international law which regulate the conduct of states as entities in their relation with one another, and those which prescribe that states grant rights and impose duties on persons within their jurisdiction, notably on their agents. Only the latter

[24] Cited in BGE 44. i. 51.

[25] BGE 44. i. 53; German: "*Und zwar ist das hierfür massgebende Völkerrecht in der Schweiz als eidgenössisches Recht zu betrachten, da es seiner Natur nach innerstaatlich allgemeine Geltung beansprucht und deshalb dem einheitlichen internen Recht gleichgestellt sein muss*".

require " by their very nature " to be enforced within states. The rule that the courts of one state shall not take jurisdiction over another state is one of the latter kind. We have, unfortunately, no other case which would substantiate this interpretation of the Dreyfuss case. It is certain, however, that the *Bundesgericht* regarded the above stated rule of customary international law as having force equal to Swiss federal law in Switzerland, and as being, in fact, part of Swiss municipal law. In the Dreyfuss case the court, therefore, applied Swiss municipal law, identical in content with a rule of customary international law.

It is interesting to note the grounds on which the *Bundesgericht* took jurisdiction in the case. The Austrian department of justice appealed to the *Bundesgericht* on the grounds that the cantonal courts had misinterpreted international law and thereby committed a denial of justice in violation of article 4 of the constitution. The case came before the *Bundesgericht* under article 113, section 3 of the constitution which gives the *Bundesgericht* jurisdiction as a constitutional court over cases in which constitutional rights have been violated by cantonal authorities. Now, article 4 contains the fundamental principle of Swiss constitutional law that every Swiss citizen is equal before the law. This article has received an extensive interpretation at the hands of the *Bundesgericht*; it has come to be regarded as constituting a constitutional guaranty against arbitrariness and denial of justice by cantonal courts.[27] The Austrian department of justice appealed to the *Bundesgericht* as a constitutional court, on the

---

[27] See Fleiner, *op. cit.*, p. 286. The article is generally invoked where a party to a suit claims that the court has misinterpreted the law, especially cantonal law which would normally not come under the supervision of the *Bundesgericht*. The term "denial of justice" is a translation of the German word "*Rechtsverweigerung*" which is applied to violations of Swiss law by the courts. It must be distinguished from the term "denial of justice" frequently used in international claims.

ground that the decision of the cantonal court of appeal, upholding the attachment of the funds belonging to Austria
was unconstitutional, in as much as it violated article 4 of the
constitution. It was claimed that the cantonal court had
acted arbitrarily by allowing Dreyfuss to sue the Austrian
department of justice, when the real defendant was the Austrian state, and furthermore, that the court had committed a
denial of justice by disregarding a rule of customary international law, viz. that foreign states are immune in municipal
courts.

The *Bundesgericht* stated that the rules of customary international law dealing with the immunity of one state in the
courts of another must in this case be deemed to be part of
Swiss federal law. Upon examination of a number of cases
decided by foreign courts, and writings of Swiss and foreign
authors, the court found that the rule of customary international law invoked by the Austrian department of justice had
not received general acceptance. As the court said, " the
rule in question cannot be recognized as having been accepted
generally and without reservations ".[28] The *Bundesgericht*
agreed with the cantonal courts that the rule that foreign
states shall be immune in municipal courts did not apply when
the foreign state had acted *jure gestionis;* it applied only
where it had acted *jure imperii.* In this case it held that the
Austrian state had acted *jure gestionis* when it had issued
bonds through a Swiss bank, and that it was, therefore, subject to the jurisdiction of the Swiss courts. The cantonal
courts had, consequently, not committed a denial of justice
and had not violated article 4 of the constitution.

In *Schinz v. Obergericht Zürich* [29] the *Bundesgericht* was
again invoked under article 4 of the constitution. It was
alleged that the *Obergericht* [30] of the canton *Zürich* had vio-

---

[28] BGE 44. i. 54.   [29] Decision of June 4, 1926; BGE 52. i. 218.

[30] Highest cantonal court.

lated the rules of customary international law pertaining to the effects of non-recognition of a foreign government. This court had rendered a decision in which it disregarded the decrees issued by the Soviet authorities in Russia, on the ground that Switzerland had not recognized Russia. The case turned on the validity of a contract made in Russia by two Swiss citizens. The contract stipulated that Bächle should make a loan to Schinz which the latter was to repay in Swiss francs within a specified time. Schinz refused to pay, alleging that the contract was invalid since it violated the Soviet laws in two respects; first, because it stipulated for a loan in excess of 10,000 rubles, second, because it provided for repayment in foreign currency. The Zürich court nevertheless declared the contract valid and ordered Schinz to repay the loan to Bächle. Schinz took the case to the *Bundesgericht*.

This court stated that the Zürich court had taken a different view regarding the validity of Soviet decrees, with respect to contracts made in Russia, than that taken by the *Bundesgericht* in *Hausner v. Banque internationale de commerce de Petrograd*,[31] where it was held that, although Switzerland had not recognized Russia, Swiss courts take cognizance of the fact that Soviet laws are in force in Russia. The *Bundesgericht* then examined foreign cases dealing with the effects of non-recognition; it found that no unanimity existed and cited a number of conflicting decisions of foreign courts, some of which were in accord with the decision of the *Obergericht* of Zürich. The Bundesgericht came to the conclusion that there existed no generally recognized rule of customary international law on the validity of the laws of an unrecognized government, with respect to contracts made

---

[31] Decision of Dec. 10, 1924; BGE 50. ii. 507. The *Bundesgericht* held that through the Soviet nationalization decrees private banks had been liquidated in Russia and had no longer any legal existence.

under the jurisdiction of that government. It, therefore, rejected the claim made by Schinz that the Zürich court had committed a denial of justice. It said:

A denial of justice, and, therefore, violation of article 4 of the constitution . . . takes place only where a clear statutory prescription or an *established, generally recognized rule of law* have been violated. . . . It cannot be said that in the case at bar a generally recognized rule of law has been violated. . . . *The case depends on a debated question of international law,* which has been differently answered in the jurisprudence of several states.[32]

In these two cases the *Bundesgericht* has held that a cantonal court commits a denial of justice, in the sense of article 4 of the constitution, when it violates a generally recognized rule of customary international law. Where it is found, through an examination of Swiss and foreign writers and court decisions that no general agreement exists on a given rule of customary international law, the *Bundesgericht* will not reverse the decision of a cantonal court on the ground of denial of justice, even when the latter has rendered a decision which conflicts with the position taken by the *Bundesgericht* in a similar case. In other words, the *Bundesgericht* will reverse the decision of a cantonal court for denial of justice only when the latter has been guilty of violating a clear statutory prescription or an established, generally recognized rule of law—either Swiss customary law or customary international law.

The *Bundesgericht* has never explained what it understands by the term " established, generally recognized rule of international law ". It has nowhere stated that such a rule must have received the acceptance of Switzerland; in both cases, although Swiss writers were cited, only foreign court

[32] Decision of June 4, 1926; BGE 52. i. 220 (italics inserted).

decisions were given, as there had been no Swiss cases. In the Dreyfuss case the court of appeal of Basel had declared that the rule of law invoked by the Austrian department of justice, viz. that states enjoyed immunity in foreign courts even for acts done *jure gestionis,* could not be accepted as an "established rule of customary international law", nor had it been "established for Switzerland by Swiss judicial precedent".[33] The Swiss courts seem to proceed on the assumption that any rule of law which has been generally accepted as a rule of customary international law must have received the assent of Switzerland. The violation of such a rule by a cantonal court is regarded as a denial of justice within the meaning of article 4 of the constitution and gives rise to an appeal to the *Bundesgericht* under article 113, section 3 of the constitution. Such a rule has been declared by the *Bundesgericht* to be part of Swiss federal law.

In a recent case, *Hellenische Republik v. Obergericht Zürich,*[34] the *Bundesgericht* reversed the decision of the Zürich court on the ground that the latter had violated a rule of customary international law.

The cantonal court had decided that property of the Greek government, deposited in a Swiss bank, could be attached for the payment of claims arising from unpaid capital and interest of bonds of a railroad corporation which had been taken over by the Greek government. The Greek government took the case to the *Bundesgericht* alleging that the

---

[33] Cited in BGE 44. i. 51. Compare the statement by Lord Alverstone in *West Rand Central Gold Mining Co. v. The King* (L. R. [1915] 2 K. B. 391): "the international law to be applied must, like anything else, be proved by satisfactory evidence, which must show either that the particular proposition put forward has been recognized and acted upon by our country, or that it is of such a nature, and has been so widely and generally accepted, that it can hardly be supposed that any civilized state would repudiate it".

[34] Decision of March 28, 1930; BGE 56. i. 237.

cantonal court had violated a rule of customary international law, and therefore article 4 of the constitution.

This case differed from the Dreyfuss case in that here the foreign government had not issued the bonds in Switzerland, nor designated any Swiss bank to pay interest on the bonds, nor in any other way subjected itself to the jurisdiction of Switzerland. The *Bundesgericht* examined a number of foreign court decisions and came to the conclusion that the courts of one state could take jurisdiction over another state only if the latter had impliedly or expressly subjected itself to the jurisdiction of the former; it found that it had never been asserted that courts could take jurisdiction over claims against a foreign government arising from transactions that had occurred wholly without the territory. It denied that the mere fact that a foreign government owned immovable property in the state would give its courts jurisdiction over such transactions, still less that it would authorize the courts to attach such property for the payment of claims arising from such transactions.

The *Bundesgericht* stressed the fact that the courts of many countries had declared themselves incompetent to entertain any suits against a foreign government, even in cases where the latter had acted *jure gestionis* and had subjected itself to the jurisdiction of the state by concluding contracts within its territory. It concluded that " in view of this situation and of the resistance which still exists in the jurisprudence of many countries and among writers even against this limited exemption from the general immunity of foreign states, Swiss jurisprudence is not justified at present to go any further ".[35] The court held that there existed a generally recognized rule of customary international law, at present, which did not permit a state to allow its courts to exercise jurisdiction over suits against another state, merely

[35] BGE 56. i. 249.

because the latter owned intangible property in the former. This rule had been violated by the cantonal court; its decision was, therefore, reversed.

This case is interesting for the light it throws on the court's attitude towards the relation of customary international law to Swiss statutes. According to article 271, section 4 of the Swiss federal bankruptcy law,[36] Swiss courts may levy an attachment against the Swiss property of debtors residing outside Switzerland. The Zürich court had attached the property of the Greek government under authorority given by this article. But the *Bundesgericht* denied that article 271 applied in this case. It stated that it was most improbable that the Swiss legislature had intended article 271 to apply to the exceptional case where the debtor was a foreign state. The court stressed the fact that, at the time when the bankruptcy law was passed, there existed general agreement in the courts of all states which had had occasion to deal with the matter that, irrespective of the nature of the action of the foreign government from which a suit against it had arisen, customary international law made it unlawful for the courts of one state to levy execution on the property of another state. This generally accepted rule had been disregarded by a few isolated Italian decisions only. The *Bundesgericht* gave great weight to the consideration that, at the time when the bankruptcy law was passed, the *Bundesrat* had declared itself in agreement with the general rule that the property of a foreign state was immune from attachment. The court referred to the protest of the *Bundesrat* against a suit brought in a French court against the canton of Geneva.[37] In the opinion of the *Bundesgericht*

---

[36] *Schuldbetreibungs- und Konkursordnung.*

[37] Suit brought by the heirs of Civry in the matter of the estate of the Duke of Brunswick (*Bundesblatt der Schweizerischen Eidgenossenschaft* (1892), part ii, p. 810).

these considerations made it clear that the legislature had not intended article 271, section 4 of the bankruptcy law to apply to foreign states. There existed, therefore, no conflict between customary international law and a Swiss statute.[38]

The few cases in which Swiss courts have indicated why they enforce rules of customary international law do not enable us to make a definite statement on the position of customary international law in Swiss courts. It is certain, however, that rules of customary international law have frequently been applied by the courts. In a few cases the *Bundesgericht* has taken jurisdiction as a constitutional court where it was alleged that, by refusing to apply a rule of customary international law, the cantonal court had committed a denial of justice within the meaning of article 4 of the constitution. A denial of justice in this sense has taken place only when the cantonal court has disregarded a " generally recognized rule of international law ".

The courts have not made it clear what is to be understood by the term " generally recognized rule of international law ". Apparently a rule which is recognized by England, America, France, Germany, but not by Italy and Belgium is not " generally recognized ". However, a rule recognized by England, America, France, Germany and Belgium, but disregarded in a few isolated Italian decisions is still " generally recognized ". Where the *Bundesrat* has expressed its view on a question of customary international law, this view apparently carries weight with the court.

[38] It may be mentioned here that immediately after the decision of the Dreyfuss case, the *Bundesrat* passed a decree under its exceptional wartime powers, forbidding the courts to levy execution against the movable property of a foreign state whenever that state grants Switzerland reciprocity; the decree gave the *Bundesrat* sole competence to determine whether reciprocity was given. (July 12, 1918, A. S. n. F. 34, 775). After the *Bundesversammlung* had rejected the draft of a bill introduced by the *Bundesrat* to give legislative effect to the provisions of the wartime decree, the decree was annulled July 8, 1926, A. S. n. F., 42, 285).

A rule which the Swiss courts declare to be " a generally recognized rule of international law " is deemed to be part of Swiss law, equal to a federal statute.   As such it would overrule cantonal law.[39]   In the case *Hellenische Republic v. Obergericht Zürich*,[40] the *Bundesgericht* interpreted a Swiss federal statute with the presumption that the legislature had not intended thereby to violate a generally recognized rule of international customary law.

[39] *Übergangsbestimmungen zur Bundesverfassung*, article 2; see Fleiner, *op. cit.*, p. 421; *supra*, p. 105.

[40] BGE 56. i. 237.

CHAPTER IV

Conclusions

In Switzerland, the treaty-making and the law-making powers are vested in one organ, the *Bundesversammlung.* Its approval of a treaty gives the treaty, upon its publication in the *Amtliche Sammlung der Bundesgesetze und Verordnungen der Schweizerischen Eidgenossenschaft,* the force of a Swiss federal law.

Treaties overrule earlier federal laws. When a federal law conflicts with an earlier treaty, Swiss courts interpret the former with the presumption that the legislature intended the treaty to remain in force as a special law alongside the more recent statute. It has never been admitted that a federal statute annulled an earlier treaty.

On the basis of the few decisions which deal with the obligatory force of customary international law in Swiss courts, the following conclusions may be ventured:

Generally recognized rules of customary international law are deemed to be part of Swiss law equal to federal statutes. Federal statutes are interpreted with the presumption that the legislature did not intend to violate a generally recognized rule of customary international law.

Treaties which have been published, and generally recognized rules of international law overrule, as part of Swiss federal law, the laws of the several cantons.

PART III

FRANCE

CHAPTER I

INTRODUCTION

FRENCH writers have not dealt with the relation between international law and municipal law, except as it presents itself in the study of the position of treaties in the courts. They have been considerably influenced by the theories of Laband and Gneist. Most French writers hold that a signed and ratified treaty, although valid in international law, requires an additional act of the government to make it obligatory on French citizens and courts.[1]

Fauchille says:

But if a treaty, ratified and registered [with the League of Nations] is perfected for the states which have signed it, it is yet necessary to make it obligatory in municipal law for citizens and subjects. This is done by publication or promulgation. . . . In France, the president of the republic usually issues a decree of promulgation which reproduces the entire treaty.[2]

The Laband-Gneist theory has recently been criticized by a number of French writers.[3] As we shall presently see,

[1] See for instance: Fauchille, *Traité de droit international public* (Paris, 1926), part i, vol. iii, no. 831; Piédelièvre, *Précis de droit international public* (Paris, 1894), vol. i, p. 298; Esmein, *Éléments de droit constitutionnel* (Paris, 1928), vol. ii, p. 207; Pillaut, *Nature juridique et effets généraux des traités internationaux* in Clunet, 1919, pp. 593, 597; Prudhomme, *La Loi territoriale et les traités internationaux* (Paris, 1910).

[2] Fauchille, *op. cit.*, p. 346.

[3] Noël, *De l'autorité des traités comparé à celle des lois* (Paris, 1922); Pillet, *Manuel de droit international privé* (Paris, 1924), vol. i, pp. 154-164; Niboyet, *Manuel de droit international privé* (Paris, 1928), p. 44; Hoijer, *Les Traités internationaux* (Paris, 1928), pp. 327 *et seq.*

their doctrines are not in accord with the practice of French courts. This is admitted by Pillet.[4] Niboyet also concedes that in certain states an additional act of the government is required to make a treaty enforceable in the courts, but denies this for France.[5] He, as well as Noël, the most ardent defender of the superiority of treaties over national laws and their immediate effects in the municipal sphere, find themselves in conflict with French practice constantly.[6] Hoijer is inconsistent when he denounces the German dualistic theories on treaties, and then states that: " an act of internal public law always intervenes to adopt a treaty into French municipal law ".[7] This is exactly what the German doctrine holds, viz. that treaties are not *ipsa lege* obligatory on municipal courts, but must be rendered internally enforceable by an act of the government.

We shall now examine the position accorded treaties in the French courts.

[4] Pillet, *op. cit.*, pp. 154-155.

[5] Niboyet, *op. cit.*, p. 44.

[6] Noël, *op. cit.*, p. 180.

[7] Hoijer, *op. cit.*, p. 360; for criticism of German theories, see: *ibid.*, pp. 327 *et seq.*

CHAPTER II

TREATIES

UNDER the absolutism of the Bourbons the treaty as well as the law-making power was vested solely in the king.[1] There existed a custom of having treaties registered by the *Parlement* of Paris; this has been interpreted as a requirement that the assent of the *Parlement* was needed for treaties. The *Parlement,* however, had no power to refuse registration of treaties; this was a mere formality which, moreover, fell into disuse after the Treaty of the Pyrenees of 1659.[2]

The numerous constitutions which France has adopted since 1791 have dealt with the conclusion of treaties in three different ways. The constitutions of 1791, 1793, *an III,* 1848 and 1870 required the approval of the legislature for all treaties.[3] This approval was regarded as a *condicio juris*

---

[1] It has been claimed that no territory could be ceded without the consent of the *États-généraux,* but Michon, *Les Traités internationaux devant les chambres,* pp. 17-26, ably refutes this theory, and shows that the kings never regarded the consent of the *États-généraux* as obligatory for treaties of cession. They asked for it, either to obtain moral support for refusing to cede territory, or on the behest of the state to which territory was ceded, because the latter regarded the consent of the *États-généraux* as an additional guarantee for the faithful execution of the treaty.

[2] Michon, *op. cit.,* p. 26.

[3] With the exception of the last, these constitutions provided for negotiation and signature of treaties by the executive, but required legislative approval before ratification could take place. From 1870-75 France had no written constitution, but sovereignty resided completely in the *Assemblée nationale* which, therefore, was the sole competent organ to conclude treaties.

for the validity of treaties in international law.[4]   The *sénatus-consulte* of 16 *therm. an* X, the constitution of the Empire of *an* XII, the royal *Chartes* of 1814 and 1830 and that of the second Empire of 1852 vested the treaty-making power in the executive.[5]   This led to difficulties, as the legislature had retained sole power to alter the laws, vote expenditures, and modify the tariff.   Treaties dealing with any of these subjects, and concluded by the executive alone, depended on the good will of the legislature for their execution. Profiting by unpleasant experiences with the royal *Chartes,* the constitutional law of February 25, 1875 chose a method for the conclusion of treaties, which was to avoid the drawbacks of those of the constitutions which virtually vested the treaty-making power in the legislature, and those which gave it to the executive alone.   The framers of the constitutional law of 1875 were strongly influenced by the constitution of Belgium of 1831, which was, at that time, considered to be a model for all constitutional governments.[6]   The constitution of Belgium had in turn been influenced by the French consular constitution of *an* VIII, the first constitution which classified treaties into those which could be concluded by the executive on his sole authority, and those which required in addition the approval of the legislature.[7]   This classifica-

[4] See Michon, *op. cit.,* p. 42.

[5] The *sénatus-consulte* of 16 *therm. an* X and the identical provision in the constitution of *an* XII gave Napoleon I power to conclude all treaties, subject only to the advice of the *Conseil privé,* and with the stipulation that they had to be communicated to the Senate before promulgation.   Since the *Conseil privé* was designated by Napoleon for each specific case, and as its advice was not compulsory, Napoleon did, in fact, conclude treaties on his sole responsibility.

[6] See Gneist, *Gutachten über die Auslegung des Paragraph 48*; appendix to E. Meier, *Über den Abschluss von Staatsverträgen* (Leipzig, 1874), p. 340.   On the Belgian constitution see *infra*, p. 198.

[7] This classification of treaties which was common to a great number of European constitutional governments before 1919, was copied from the Belgian constitution, but actually goes back to the French consular constitution of *an* VIII.   See *infra*, p. 197.

tion of treaties was adopted in article 8 of the constitutional law of 1875. Article 8 reads as follows:

The President of the Republic negotiates and ratifies treaties. He presents them to the Chambers as soon as the interest and the security of the state permit thereof. Treaties of peace and commerce, and treaties which involve the finances of the state, and those relating to the status of persons and property rights of French citizens abroad are not valid [8] until voted upon by the two Chambers. No alienation, no exchange, and no acquisition of territory can take place except by virtue of a law.

Negotiation, signature and ratification of all treaties is left to the president, but for certain treaties he must obtain the assent of the legislature. The approval of a treaty by the legislature takes the form of a law authorizing the president to ratify. Reference by French courts to " ratification " of treaties by the legislature is incorrect; [9] the legislature merely authorizes ratification, the president ratifies.

Under the 1875 constitution the president concludes on his sole authority [10] the following kinds of treaties: Political treaties, such as alliances, armistices, peace settlements in colonial wars, establishments of pseudo-protectorates, also temporary treasury settlements, treaties relating to the status of foreigners in France and extradition treaties. The approval of the Chambers is required for treaties of peace and commerce, treaties providing for a draft on the treasury— such as treaties stipulating for loans or acknowledging debts —postal, telegraph and parcel post conventions, treaties dealing with personal and property rights of French citizens

[8] The French term is "*ne sont définitifs*".

[9] See, for example, the case of *Pratt v. Lycett*, D. 1892. 2. 593; *infra,* p. 138.

[10] Every *acte* (official instrument in writing) of the president must be countersigned by a minister; in the case of treaties, the minister of foreign affairs (art. 3 of the constitutional law of February 25, 1875).

abroad, conventions on literary, artistic and industrial property, and treaties providing for alienation, exchange or acquisition of territory.[11]   Although not required to do so by article 8, the government submits treaties modifying legislation to the Chambers.   This is done partly for political reasons—to gain the support of the Chambers for the government's foreign policy—partly, also, to assure the enforcement of the treaty in the courts.   As we shall presently see, French courts have been reluctant to admit that a treaty concluded by the executive alone could modify a law.[12]

Where the constitution made the assent of the legislature a *condicio juris* for the international validity of all treaties, as in most revolutionary constitutions, no question could arise whether these treaties could be enforced internally. The assent of the legislature was given in the form of a law, duly promulgated and published, and was as such obligatory on citizens and courts.

Where the constitution, however, vested the treaty-making power exclusively in the executive, as in the constitutions of

---

[11] Moreau, *Précis élémentaire de droit constitutionnel* (Paris, 1897), p. 321, and Clunet, " *Du défaut de validité de plusieurs traités diplomatiques conclus par la France avec les puissances étrangères* ", in Cl. 1880, 5, maintain that the enumeration in article 8 is intended to include all treaties, as in the First and Second Republic all treaties had to be approved by the legislature. This view is not accepted today. Michon, *op. cit.*, pp. 228-235; Hoijer, *op. cit.*, pp. 84-120; Esmein, *Éléments du droit constitutionnel* (Paris, 1928), vol. ii, p. 200; Renault, " *De la conclusion des traités internationaux* ", in *Le Droit*, May 26, 1880, hold that the president is empowered to conclude treaties on his sole authority, with the exception of those enumerated in article 8 for which he has to obtain the approval of the legislature. This has been the practice of the government and appears to be in accord with the text of article 8. Furthermore, the first draft, modelled after the 1848 constitution, had been rejected because it vested the treaty-making power in the legislature; article 8 was evidently intended to limit the powers of the legislature in a manner similar to that adopted by the Belgian constitution of 1831.

[12] *Infra*, pp. 140-147.

1814, 1830 and 1852, the question arose whether the treaty-making power extended the prerogatives of the executive into fields ordinarily reserved to the legislature, such as law-making, modification of the tariff, public expenditures, or, on the other hand, whether the provisions of the constitution which restrained the power of the executive generally applied also to the exercise of his treaty-making power. In the latter case, he would be authorized to conclude, without the approval of the Chambers, only treaties dealing with subjects which he could normally regulate by means of decrees; all those treaties which dealt with subjects reserved to the legislature, would, however, require its approval. The question was never authoritatively solved and gave rise to conflicts between executive and legislature which proved to be embarrassing for France.[18] To avoid international complications,

[18] Especially the serious situation which arose in 1834 when the Chambers refused to vote the necessary funds to pay to the United States the indemnity specified in the treaty of July 4, 1831, in settlement of the French spoliation claims. The United States had drawn a check on the French treasury for the first instalment; this was not honored. The United States protested energetically and the French government found itself in a most embarrassing position. Finally the Chambers capitulated, adding to the law which appropriated the necessary sums a rebuke to the government, for not having obtained their approval prior to ratification of the treaty (*Moniteur universel*, March 29, 1835, p. 659; see Moore, *A Digest of International Law*, vol. v, pp. 231-232).

An extensive discussion on the subject of the treaty-making power of the executive occurred on April 18, 1826, in connection with the treaty with England of Jan. 26, 1826. In this treaty certain modifications of the tariffs were agreed upon. The Chambers passed a resolution in which they asserted the right to refuse to pass the laws necessary for carrying into effect treaties dealing with subjects reserved to them. The right of the executive to conclude such treaties was, however, acknowledged (*Moniteur universel*, April 20, 1826, p. 508). The resolution recognized the possibility of a conflict between international validity and internal execution of treaties. In this particular case, however, the minister of finance succeeded in convincing the Chambers that the treaty had not stipulated for new duties, but had actually lowered the duties to be paid by French ships.

the king, when ratifying the Treaty of London of May 7, 1832, merely promised to ask for a vote of the Chambers for the financial measures therein contained.[14]

Napoleon III, however, concluded the treaty of commerce with Sardinia of 1852 without asking for the assent of the legislature, although this treaty modified the tariff. He then asked the Senate for an interpretation of article 6 of the constitution of 1852, with regard to treaties of commerce modifying the tariff. The *sénatus-consulte* of Dec. 23-30, 1852, declared that " the treaties of commerce made by virtue of article 6 of the constitution have the force of law for modifications of the tariff which they stipulate ".[15] This interpretation of article 6 by the Senate was restricted to treaties of commerce modifying the tariff, because the question was limited to such treaties. There seems to be no reason why treaties modifying legislation, concluded under the 1852 constitution, should not be considered as having force of law also.[16] The Senate evidently regarded article 6 as restricting the powers ordinarily reserved to the legislature.[17]

We shall see, however, that French courts were reluctant to enforce the treaties concluded by Napoleon III without the approval of the Chambers, when these treaties modified the laws.[18]

To avoid conflicts between executive and legislature over

[14] The treaty provided for the guarantee of a Greek loan. See De Clercq, *Recueil des traités de la France* (Paris, 1864-   ), vol. iv, p. 179; see also *ibid.*, vol. xiv, p. 188.

[15] Article 3. Under Art. 27 of the constitution the Senate was authorized to interpret the constitution.

[16] This is the opinion of Demangeat, " *Les Dispositions des différents codes ne peuvent-elles être modifiées que par une loi et non par un traité diplomatique?* " Cl. 1874, p. 107.

[17] The most important treaty of commerce of the whole reign of Napoleon III, that of Jan. 23, 1860 with England, was concluded without the assent of the Chambers.

[18] *Infra*, pp. 140-147.

the internal execution of treaties, the constitution of 1875 stipulated that certain treaties require the assent of the legislature. This assent is given in the form of a law, duly promulgated and published, and as such becomes obligatory on citizens and courts. The vote of the Chambers is regularly obtained before ratification; it authorizes the president to ratify the treaty. It is, in other words, a *condicio juris* for the international validity of the treaty.[19]

French courts have regularly held that it is promulgation by the executive which makes treaties obligatory on them.[20]

The *Cour de cassation* [21] first expressed itself clearly on

[19] It is not specified in article 8 of the constitutional law of 1875 that treaties modifying legislation require legislative approval, but they are wisely submitted by the government to the Chambers. The Chambers are not inclined to take advantage of the constitutional defects of signed and ratified treaties as this would compromise France internationally. This was evident in the debates on Nov. 4, 1890 (*Journal officiel*, Nov. 4, 1890, p. 1884; see Michon, *op. cit.*, p. 201) with regard to the Anglo-French treaty of Paris of Aug. 4, 1889 for the delimitation of colonial possessions on the West coast of Africa. The treaty had not been submitted to the Chambers and, as it referred to " exchange of territory ", they were justified in attacking its constitutionality. However, they renounced this constitutional right, in order to present a united front in foreign policy.

The different terminology of the last sentence of article 8 seems to be that territory might conceivably be acquired without a treaty (in uncivilized countries). So held by Michon, *op. cit.*, pp. 240-245; Hoijer, *op. cit.*, pp. 97-104. Possibly, however, this provision was taken over bodily from the Belgian constitution, where the different terminology of the last sentence was closely related to the provisions of article 3 of the Belgian constitution (see *infra*, p. 198). There is, at any rate, no difference in the action of the Chambers when they approve treaties of cession, alienation or exchange of territory, from that when they approve other treaties requiring legislative assent.

[20] In France, laws must have been promulgated before they become " obligatory " on courts and private persons (article 1 of the civil code; constitutional law of July 16, 1875, art. 7, sec. 1).

[21] The *Cour de cassation* is the highest French court; it sits at Paris and is composed of a president-in-chief, three presidents for its three chambers (criminal, civil and *requêtes*) and 45 justices, all appointed

this matter, Nov. 28, 1834, in the case of *Jauge, Tassin et autres*. Certain Frenchmen had assisted Don Carlos of Spain who had by the Treaty of the Quadruple Alliance of 1834 been declared a public enemy. The treaty had not yet been promulgated. The accused were acquitted by the court because " the treaty of April 22, 1834 has not been promulgated in France; it can, therefore, not lawfully become the basis of a judicial prosecution ".[22]

In the case *Société anglo-française de Saint-Gaudens,* the *Cour de cassation* re-affirmed this principle. In considering the Anglo-French treaty of 1862, which gave corporations the right to plead before the courts of the two countries, the court said that "the treaty . . . having been sanctioned and promulgated May 17, 1862, has *by virtue of this promulgation* become executory in France ".[23]

Again in the case *Yter v. Administration des douanes,* the same court held that " treaties regularly promulgated in France *have the force of law,* and must *for this reason* be applied by the judicial authorities.[24] [25]

for life by the executive. It reviews questions of law only. It does not substitute its own decision for that of the lower court, but either affirms or reverses it; in the latter case the case is sent back to another court of the same rank as that from which the erroneous decision came, for redetermination of the matter. This court may refuse to abide by the interpretation given by the *Cour de cassation;* the case can then again be brought to the *Cour de cassation* and if it is again annulled, the third court must abide by the ruling of the *Cour de cassation.*

[22] S. 1834. 1. 822; the treaty was promulgated Dec. 9, 1834.

[23] Decision of May 19, 1863; S. 1863. 1. 353. (Italics inserted.)

[24] Decision of July 27, 1877; S. 1877. 1. 485 (italics inserted). See also *Cour de cassation,* Jan. 10, 1842; S. 1842. 1. 236; *Tribunal civil* of Lyons, June 5, 1884, Cl. 1885, 85; *Cour d'appel* of Paris, April 11, 1892; D. 1892. 2. 593; *Cour d'appel* of Rouen, June 26, 1900; Cl. 1901, 359, 370. Whereas in Belgium only treaties which have received legislative approval are promulgated, in France all treaties are promulgated. See *infra,* p. 207.

[25] The *Tribunal civil* is a court of first instance dealing with civil matters; in penal matters it sits as a *Tribunal correctionnel.* These tribunals

To support his theory that no transformation of a treaty is required to make it internally obligatory, Noël claims that the *Cour de cassation* confused promulgation and publication in the case of *Jauge Tassin et autres,* and continued to make the same mistake in later decisions.[26] He admits that treaties must be published before they can be enforced in the courts, because they must be known to private persons. By conceding the necessity of publication, he admits that the fact that a treaty is ratified and therefore internationally binding does not alone suffice to make it enforceable in the courts; the act of publication is necessary to render it obligatory in municipal law. Furthermore, his argument that it is publication and not promulgation which is required to give the treaty force of law in the courts is purely academic. As Esmein points out: " The promulgation and the publication coincide in fact, as it is by the publication of the decree of promulgation that a law is published ".[27] The same is true for treaties. With respect to the nature of promulgation, Esmein says: " The promulgation is the act by which the chief of the executive power . . . gives to the agents of the state the order to see that [a law] is obeyed and enforced ".[28]

are composed of a varying number of judges, appointed for life. They sit in first and last instance in certain civil cases involving not less than 600 francs nor more than 1500. In other cases their decisions are subject to appeal before the *Cours d'appel.*

The *Cours d'appel* are also composed of judges appointed for life. The number of such courts is determined by statute. They hear appeals from the tribunals of first instance and the commercial tribunals.

The *Tribunaux commercials* are elective tribunals composed of a varying number of judges elected by merchants and mariners from among qualified voters of thirty years of age, and French merchants of the district. They hear cases involving commercial and banking transactions and bankruptcy. Their decisions are subject to appeal before the *Cours d'appel.*

[26] Noël, *op. cit.,* p. 138.   [27] Esmein, *op. cit.,* p. 68.

[28] *Ibid.,* p. 68; see also Duguit, *Manuel de droit constitutionnel* (Paris, 1923), p. 306. The term " agents of the state " includes courts.

In view of the repeated statements of the *Cour de cassation* that it is promulgation which makes a treaty internally executory and enforceable in the courts, we feel justified in rejecting Noël's theory that treaties are *eo ipso* obligatory in municipal law. After a treaty has become internationally binding on France, this additional act of the government—the promulgation of the treaty—is required to give it force of law in French municipal law. This view of the French courts is in harmony with the Laband-Gneist theory.[29]

Treaties have force of law in France from date of promulgation. In *Dame Hotermans v. liquid. Nortz,* the *Tribunal civil* of Havre held that: " A treaty . . . is a law which does not become obligatory on private persons until its promulgation ".[30]

It will prove helpful for an understanding of the attitude of the courts in cases where a treaty conflicts with a previously enacted law, if we briefly state the French doctrine regarding the application of laws and decrees by the courts.

The courts have no authority to examine the constitutionality of laws, regularly promulgated by decree of the executive. This is a result of the principle expressed in article 3, chapter V, title III of the constitution of 1791 : " The courts are forbidden to interfere with the exercise of the legislative power, or to suspend the execution of laws." This principle is in force today. Furthermore, article 10, title II of the law of Aug. 17, 1790 stated: " The courts are forbidden to . . . hinder or suspend the execution of acts of the legislature ".[31]

---

[29] Courts must take judicial notice of treaties; see Bartin, *Principes de droit international privé* (Paris, 1930), p. 98; *Cour de cassation*, July 15, 1811 ; S. 1811. 1. 301.

[30] Decision of June 4, 1920. *Revue de droit international privé et de droit pénal international* (1921), p. 465; also S. 1863. 1. 353; *infra,* p. 145.

[31] Esmein, *op. cit.*, vol. i, p. 592; Duguit, op. cit., p. 305; Recently Duguit, *op. cit.,* p. 306; Jèze and Berthélemy, in *Revue de droit inter-*

On the other hand, French courts have the right to examine the legality of administrative ordinances and of the decrees of the president.[32] These must be within the powers granted by the law which authorizes them. The basis for this right of review is found in article 471, no. 15 of the penal code, which speaks of ordinances " *légalement faits* " and allows penal sanctions only for these. An extensive interpretation has applied this provision to all ordinances and decrees.[33]

As we have seen, it is the decree of promulgation which renders treaties enforceable in the courts. The promulgation of treaties which have received legislative approval differs in no way from that of all laws passed by the legislature. The law authorizing the president to ratify is promulgated together with the text of the treaty. These treaties fulfill all the constitutional requirements for the passage of laws and are regarded by the courts as equivalent to laws. They may, therefore, not be examined by the courts as to their legality, but must be applied according to the maxim *lex posterior derogat priori.*

On the other hand, treaties which have not received legislative approval derive their authority in French municipal law solely from the presidential decree of promulgation. They resemble, therefore, decrees rather than statutes, unless the constitution invests them with the force of statutes. If they have only force of decrees, the courts would be entitled to examine their legality and to refuse to apply them when they conflict with laws. We shall see that French courts have been reluctant to allow treaties, concluded without the

national public (1912), p. 139, have argued for the right of judicial review of laws, but there has been no change in practice.

[32] All acts of the president are called decrees (*décrets*); those of the kings under the 1814 and 1830 constitutions were called ordinances (*ordonnances*); see Duguit, *op. cit.*, p. 506.

[33] Duguit, *op. cit.*, p. 305.

approval of the legislature, to modify laws. It is suggested that this hesitancy is due to the uncertainty with regard to the character of these treaties, viz. whether they have force of laws or only force of decrees.[34]

Where treaties, for which the approval of the legislature had been obtained, conflicted with previously enacted laws, the courts have regularly applied the treaties:

On April 11, 1892, the *Cour d'appel* of Paris rendered its decision in the well-known case *Pratt v. Lycett*. These were the facts of the case:

An American had bought the rights to an invention and received a patent in the United States. He subsequently applied and received a patent in France, and instituted suit against a French firm for encroaching on his patent rights. The French firm replied that he had manufactured and sold his articles in France before having obtained the patent, and could, consequently, according to the law of 1844, not receive a French patent. It was argued on behalf of plaintiff, however, that this law had been superseded by the Convention of Paris for the Protection of Industrial Property of 1883. This treaty provided that articles patented in one of the signatory states could, pending the granting of a patent in another signatory state, be manufactured and sold in the latter state during a period of twelve months. The court applied the treaty of 1883 stating that:

This treaty has been ratified by the legislative power in France [35] (Senate, June 30, 1883; Chamber of deputies, Jan. 19, 1884). It has *therefore* force of law. The argument that it is not valid, because it exceeds the powers accorded the president in article

[34] In Belgium, treaties concluded without the assent of the legislature are frankly considered as having the force of decrees only, and the courts will not enforce them when they conflict with laws. See *infra*, p. 203.

[35] This statement is incorrect; the legislature authorizes the president to ratify, but it is the president who ratifies. See *supra*, p. 129.

8 must be rejected. . . . By approving the treaty, *the legislature has made a true law thereof which is obligatory on everybody [in France]*.[36]

In the case *Fillinger v. Préfet de la Loire* the *Tribunal civil* of Montbrizon stated that " *the treaty* of May 10, 1871, ratified by the national assembly, *has the force of law* and must be applied even when it is not in conformity with the civil code." [37]

An interesting case came before the *Conseil de revision de la VIIme armée* on May 6, 1918. A German prisoner by the name of Krug had attempted to escape in the uniform of an American soldier; he was caught and condemned to death in accordance with article 207 of the code of military justice, which punishes any enemy found in the war zone in disguise as a spy. The case was appealed to the *Conseil de revision* on the ground that articles 8 and 29 of the Hague Conventions of 1899 and 1907 declare that to constitute " espionage " there must be evidence that the enemy intended to procure information and to communicate it to the opposite party. It was argued that the definition of a " spy " adopted in the Hague conventions must be accepted by the tribunal in preference to that of the code of military justice. Asked for an interpretation of the Hague conventions in question,[38] the

---

[36] *D.* 1892. 2. 593 (italics inserted). The court here held that a treaty which had received the approval of the legislature overruled an earlier French law.

[37] Decision of Jan. 25, 1877; Cl. 1877, 43 (italics inserted).

[38] Article 8 and 29 of the 1907 convention merely restated articles 8 and 29 of the 1899 convention. The *Conseil de Revision* was asked to reverse the decision of the lower military court because of violation of the 1907 convention. Since articles 8 and 29 of the 1907 convention merely restated those of the 1899 convention they did not fall under the " general participation clause ", and were binding on the court if not as provisions of the 1907, then as provisions of the 1899 Hague conventions. (See Garner, *International Law and the World War* (London, 1920), pp. 19-20).

minister of foreign affairs declared that: " Article 29 [of the Hague Convention of 1907] determines alone, to the exclusion of the municipal law, the facts which constitute espionage ".[39]   The decision imposing the death penalty was reversed and a disciplinary penalty decreed.

The cases cited show that the courts were willing to enforce treaties, concluded with the approval of the legislature, even when they conflicted with existing laws.   Where treaties for which legislative approval had not been obtained conflicted with previous laws, we find a much less precise and consistent jurisprudence.   The courts usually interpret the treaty strictly in order to harmonize it with the law. The national law is generally favored.

On June 24, 1839 the *Cour de cassation* was called upon to decide whether the peace treaty of May 30, 1814, by which the confiscated possessions of the Duke of Richmond [40] were returned to his heirs, stipulated that the *droit d'aubaine* should regulate the succession.   France had abolished primogeniture and the court held that the treaty had merely restored the property to the heirs of the original owner, but had not regulated the succession in a manner contrary to French law.   The court said:

If the text of that provision left any doubt as to its true meaning, this doubt would be dispelled by the rules of law on the interpretation of treaties; the first is to find the common intention of the contracting parties, rather than to follow the literal sense of the terms employed.   It is impossible to suppose that it was the intention of the plenipotentiaries to regulate the laws of succession. . . . Diplomatic treaties must be understood in the sense which harmonizes them with the civil and public law of the contracting states; the interpretation of the treaty by the

[39] *Affaire Krug*; Cl. 1919, 1108.

[40] The decree of Berlin of Oct. 21, 1806 had ordered that the property of Englishmen in France be sequestered.

lower court gives a meaning to the treaty which places it into opposition with all the rules of French civil and public law.[41]

In interpreting the treaty, the court primarily sought to harmonize it with existing French law, rather than to find the common intention of the contracting parties, notwithstanding its statement to the contrary.

In *Homberg v. Consul d'Autriche* the *Tribunal civil de la Seine* interpreted the consular treaty with Austria strictly, in order to avoid its coming in conflict with provisions of French law.[42] It was claimed that the consular treaty of 1866 gave to the Austrian consul the guardianship over the minor son of an Austrian and a Frenchwoman. After the death of her husband, the Frenchwoman had, in accordance with French law, regained her French citizenship, by reason of her residence in France. French law makes the widow the guardian of her minor children. The court held that where a conflict existed between French law and foreign law (Austrian law in this case) on a point concerning the paternal power, in other words the public order, French law must prevail. It then examined the treaty and found that:

This rule, which follows from the principle of territorial sovereignty, has not been modified by the treaty between France and Austria of Dec. 11, 1866, which gives the consuls of the

[41] *Napier et autres v. Duc de Richmond*, S. 1839. 1. 577; see also for cases where the courts interpreted treaties with a view to harmonizing them with French laws: *Cour de cassation*, Aug. 11, 1841; S. 1841. 1. 847; *Cour de cassation*, July 18, 1859; D. 1859. 1. 325; *Cour d'appel* of Amiens November 26, 1891; D. 1892. 2. 428. Bartin explains this tendency of the courts to supplement and interpret treaties by reference to French laws as a consequence of the fact that they regard treaties as equivalent to laws. (*Principes de droit international privé* (Paris, 1930), p. 105).

[42] This case is occasionally cited as showing a clear refusal of the court to apply a treaty conflicting with a prior French law. As a matter of fact, the court merely interpreted the treaty strictly; it must, however, be admitted that in so doing it strongly favored the national law.

two states primarily rights of supervision and administration for the conservation of property rights of their countrymen.[43]

In *Six et Cie. v. Opsomer* the *Cour d'appel* of Douai interpreted the Franco-Belgian treaty of 1912, which regulated the transmission of judicial acts, as not dealing with procedure. The court held that procedural matters remained governed by the municipal law of each state, in France by the code of civil procedure. The case has sometimes been quoted as showing a refusal of the court to apply a treaty which conflicted with a French law, viz. the code of civil procedure. However, as in the case *Homberg v. Consul d'Autriche,* the court succeeded in harmonizing law and treaty by interpreting the latter strictly. Its interpretation of the treaty does not appear to differ essentially from that expressed by the minister of justice in a circular dealing with this treaty.[44] Although it found no conflict between treaty and law, the court declared that " the prescriptions of article 69 [of the code of procedure] are rules which apply in all cases and *which can only be modified by a special law;* the Franco-Belgian treaty of 1912, approved by a simple decree, could not have this effect ".[45]

The Franco-Belgian treaty of 1912 was one of those which under article 8 of the 1875 constitution could be concluded by the president without obtaining the assent of the legislature. The dictum of the court seems to indicate that it would not have applied the treaty, even if the treaty had purported to regulate procedure in a way different from that of the code of civil procedure. The court is evidently reluctant to admit that a treaty concluded by the president alone can modify a law. This attitude appears to be due to the

[43] Decision of April 5, 1884; Cl. 1884, 521.

[44] Cl. 1927, 119.

[45] Cl. 1927, 119; decision of March 2, 1926 (italics inserted) see criticism in Noël, *op. cit.*, p. 153; and Perroud, note to Cl. 1927, 119.

fact that the court feels that such treaties resemble decrees rather than laws, and, of course, a decree cannot modify a law in France. The language of the court shows the wisdom of the government in regularly obtaining legislative approval for all treaties which modify laws, even where this is not expressly required by article 8 of the constitution of 1875.[46]

There have been two cases where the courts have flatly refused to apply a treaty, because it modified a previously enacted French law. In both cases the treaties had not received legislative approval:

In the case of *Sabater* the *Tribunal civil de la Seine* decided that, despite the consular treaty of 1862 with Spain, which procured for the nationals of both states equal rights in the courts, Sabater, a Spaniard, who had instituted suit against a Frenchman, was required to furnish security for costs; this may, according to French law, be demanded from any foreign plaintiff if the defendant so desires. The court declared that: " The dispositions of the different codes cannot be modified *except by a law*; it does not appear that the clause [of the treaty] cited by Sabater has been sanctioned or decreed by law ".[47]

This case has been severely criticized, particularly by Demangeat.[48] However, the cases which he cites to prove that other treaties concluded under the constitution of 1852 were applied by the courts even though they modified laws, are not in point, since in these cases no conflict existed between treaty and law.[49] On the other hand, his arguments are convincing with respect to the meaning of the *sénatus-*

[46] See *supra*, p. 130.

[47] Decision of Feb. 5, 1874; Cl. 1874, 107 (italics inserted).

[48] Cl. 1874, 107.

[49] He cites D. 1859. 1. 325; D. 1868. 1. 313; D. 1867. 1. 80; D. 1871. 2. 11. In none of these cases were the courts called upon to decide a conflict between a treaty and a previously enacted French law.

consulte of 1852 [50] which expressly stated that treaties of commerce, modifying the tariff, had the force of laws. This interpretation of article 6 by the Senate leads logically to the conclusion that all treaties concluded under the 1852 constitution have the force of laws rather than of decrees and must, consequently, be applied according to the maxim *lex posterior derogat priori.*[51]

In *Pillon v. Peck* the *Tribunal civil* of Meaux refused to enforce the treaty with the United States of 1853, on the ground that it conflicted with the French law of July 14, 1819. This law stipulates that where French and foreign heirs succeed to the same estate, the French heirs may deduct from the French portion of the estate a share equal to that from which they are excluded in the foreign portion of the estate, by reason of local laws or customs. The treaty of 1852 provided that in cases of succession the citizens of one country were to be accorded national treatment in the courts of the other. The court applied the law of 1819 to the case, stating that: " It cannot be admitted that a diplomatic treaty can abrogate a law made in favor of the French ".[52]

In two cases, French courts enforced treaties although it was claimed that they conflicted with French laws. The

[50] See *supra,* p. 132.

[51] See *supra,* p. 132.

[52] Decision of May 4, 1928; Cl. 1928, 1223. The court admitted that the law of 1819 was manifestly contrary to modern principles of conflict of laws, but held that it must, nevertheless, be applied, until the legislature would remove this discrepancy between French law and international private law. In two other cases the law of 1819 was applied despite treaties (not approved by the legislature!) : *Cour de cassation,* decision of July 18, 1859; D. 1859. 1. 325, *Vanoni v. Moineau*; *Tribunal civil de la Seine,* April 26, 1910; Cl. 1911, 254, *Melgarejo v. Mitchell et autres.* In both cases the courts succeeded, however, in interpreting the treaties in a manner which harmonized them with the 1819 law. In *Vanoni v. Moineau* the *Tribunal de la Seine* called the 1819 law the "public and international law of France" (D. 1859. 1. 327).

courts did not admit that the laws had been superseded by the subsequent treaties, but sought to harmonize them; this they did by showing that treaty and law regulated different subjects and did not, therefore, conflict. It is evident in the reasoning of the courts that they wished to avoid conflicts between treaties, which have not been approved by the legislature, and prior laws. We have seen that where the treaties had received legislative approval, the courts admitted that they could supersede French laws.[53]

In *Société anglo-francaise de Saint Gaudens* the *Cour de cassation* applied the Anglo-French convention of 1862 which stipulated that the corporations of one state could plead in the courts of the other. The law of May 30, 1857 stipulated that foreign corporations must obtain an imperial decree before they are allowed to plead in French courts. The court held that it was not necessary to obtain the imperial decree stipulated in the law of 1857, since this law was applicable only to the cases which it specifically enumerated and not to those regulated by the treaty. With respect to the obligatory force of the treaty in French municipal law, the court said: " The treaty concluded between France and England of April 30, 1862, sanctioned and promulgated May 17, 1862, has, by reason of this promulgation, become executory and therefore binding on the French courts and citizens as from that date ".[54]

In *Dolivo v. Faure* the *Tribunal civil* of Lyons found that the treaty of commerce with Switzerland of 1869, though dealing with procedural matters, did not conflict with the code of civil procedure, because the treaty regulated the procedure for executing judgments of one state in the other,

[53] *Supra*, pp. 138-140.

[54] Decision of May 19, 1863; S. 1863. 1. 353. It was pointed out by counsel for the English corporation that the law of 1853 gave the same power to the emperor which he exercised in the treaty, and that, consequently, he was free to choose the method which seemed best suited.

while the code of civil procedure regulated entirely different matters.   Treaty and code were thus harmonized.[55]

In one case the *Cour de cassation* held that a treaty, concluded without the approval of the legislature, could supersede a French law.   This was the famous case *Affaire Grus*, which dealt with the introduction of two of Donizetti's operas into France in 1887.   French law accorded a longer copyright limit than Italian law.   By the law of 1852 foreign authors were given the same rights in France, which they would have enjoyed there, had their works been published in France.   The treaty of 1862 with Sardinia, however, provided that the authors of one state should be accorded in the other state those rights only which they enjoy in their own country.   The heirs of Donizetti, wishing to avail themselves of the longer copyright limit in French law, claimed that the law of 1852 could not be superseded by the treaty of 1862 which had not received legislative approval. The *Cour de cassation*, however, said that it could, and that a special rule in a treaty might supersede a general municipal law preceding it.[56]

With respect to conflicts between treaties and previously enacted French laws, we come to the conclusion that French courts regard treaties which have received legislative approval and which have been duly promulgated as being equivalent to French statutes; they, consequently, supersede earlier statutes.

French courts are apparently uncertain whether treaties which have not received legislative approval are equivalent to statutes, or whether they do not rather resemble decrees. With the exception of the dictum of the *Cour d'appel* of *Douai* in the case *Six et Cie. v. Opsomer*,[57] all the cases which have been cited as favoring the French law—either

---

[55] Decision of June 5, 1884; Cl. 1885, 85.

[56] S. 1888. 1. 17.   [57] Cl. 1927, 119.

entirely disregarding the treaty, as in the cases *Sabater* [58] and *Pillon v. Peck*,[59] or by interpreting the treaty strictly in order to harmonize it with the French law — dealt with treaties concluded by Napoleon III under the constitution of 1852. If we compare this uncertain jurisprudence with the decisions of the courts in similar conflicts between laws and later treaties, where the latter had been concluded under the constitution of 1875 and had received legislative approval, we are driven to the conclusion that treaties over-rule prior French statutes only when they have the character of French statutes. Despite the *sénatus-consulte* of 1852,[60] the courts are reluctant to regard them as equivalent to statutes, unless the legislature has given its approval.[61] The binding force of treaties on France in international law does not concern the courts at all.[62]

When a treaty conflicts with a subsequent municipal statute, it is important to distinguish between the consequences of this conflict in international law and those in municipal law. It is generally agreed that a state cannot free itself from its treaty obligations by enacting conflicting municipal laws. In the sphere of international law such municipal laws are ineffective and the treaty remains in force. There is less agreement as to the validity of such municipal laws in the courts of the state which has enacted them.

[58] Cl. 1874, 107.

[59] Cl. 1928, 1223.

[60] See *supra*, p. 132.

[61] Since 1875, the French government submits treaties which modify laws to the Chambers, even where this is not required by article 8 of the constitution of 1875. This practice serves to avoid, for treaties concluded by the Third Republic, the uncertain position in the courts, which the treaties concluded under the Second Empire hold.

[62] This attitude of the French courts shows that French practice is in accord with the German "dualist" theory of treaties; the sole concern of the courts is with the obligatory force of treaties in French municipal law.

Pillet argues that " laws cannot overrule treaties . . . this would evidently be contrary to all law ".[63]   He, as well as Noël, believe in the supremacy of treaties over national laws, but do not distinguish between their supremacy in the sphere of international law and in that of municipal law.   The preceding discussion of the position of treaties in the courts has shown that when treaties have received the approval of the legislature and have been promulgated, they are regarded as equivalent to French laws.   Being laws, it would seem that they could be overruled by a subsequent munipical law.   This is admitted by Pillet, who says:

It is possible that, in fact, a legislature may pass a law which is not in accord with the provisions of a treaty, and expressly order the judges to apply the law.   Must the judges obey?   The question is rather embarrassing.   In a country such as ours, it seems that the judges, even if they be convinced of the irregularity of the law in its application to relations already regulated by a treaty must, nevertheless, follow the will of the legislature which is imposed on them.[64]

The reason why the judges must follow the later law, is without question the fact that in the municipal sphere the treaty has no greater legal force than the statute.

A review of the cases which came before French courts, involving conflicts between treaties and subsequent laws, will prove the correctness of the doctrine of the " dualists " that, regardless of international consequences, courts will apply later laws.

Pillaut, who maintains that courts will not apply laws which conflict with prior treaties,[65] bases his belief on the

----

[63] Pillet, *Manuel de droit international privé* (Paris, 1924), vol. i, pp. 158-159.

[64] Pillet, *op. cit.*, p. 160.   He feels that this situation is due to the principle of the separation of powers which does not permit the courts to review the legality of a duly promulgated law.

[65] Cl. 1919, 592 *et seq.*

case *Milani v. ministère public* which was decided by the *Cour de cassation* on March 6, 1897. Milani was born in Nice prior to March 24, 1860, at which date the treaty of cession was signed by which Nice became French. The treaty provided that the inhabitants of the ceded territory should attain to French citizenship, unless they declared their intention to remain Sardinian within one year. On June 30, 1860, a decree was issued to put into effect the provisions of the treaty. The decree stipulated that children born in Nice before the cession took place could claim French citizenship one year after their majority, by making a declaration to that effect. Milani had not made this declaration. The case depended on his citizenship.

It was argued that the decree referred to a class of persons not dealt with in the treaty, viz. those whose parents had not been born in Nice. Milani's father came from Tuscany, and it was, therefore, claimed that the decree applied in his case. It was not maintained that the decree superseded the treaty; the contention was that the treaty referred solely to inhabitants of Nice whose parents had been born there, and the decree to children of parents who had not been born in Nice. The court rejected this narrow interpretation of the treaty and said:

This distinction [according to the place of birth of the parent] is not expressed in the text of either decree or treaty; it is, therefore, entirely arbitrary. Furthermore, by excluding from article 6 [of the treaty] a class of persons who are clearly comprised in the generality of its terms, and from whom appellants would take away their French citizenship, they attach an illegality to the decree of June 30, 1860. This decree could not and did not intend to violate the rights acquired by the treaty of March 24, 1860.[66]

The court found no conflict between the treaty and the

[66] Cl. 1897, 559.

decree which was issued to put the provisions of the treaty
into effect. Even had there been a conflict, the case would
not be in point. All it said was that a decree could not
supersede a treaty. The case was decided a few years after
the *Affaire Grus,* in which the *Cour de cassation* had
declared that the treaty of 1862 with Sardinia had the force
of law in France, and could, therefore, supersede a French
law.[67] The treaty of cession of 1860, as well as the treaty of
1862 with Sardinia had been concluded under the constitution of 1852. They had, consequently, not received the
approval of the legislature. Nevertheless, the *Cour de cassation* had in the *Affaire Grus* taken the view that treaties
concluded under the 1852 constitution had the force of law.
As laws they could, naturally, not be superseded by a decree.

Pillet [68] cites two cases dealing with the transmission of
judicial acts by letters rogatory, to prove that courts will not
apply the later law if it conflicts with a treaty. The Franco-
Sardinian treaties of 1760 and 1860 had stipulated this procedure, but in the meantime the procedure had been simpli-
fied in both countries. The courts held that in order to avail
oneself of the advantages of the treaties, their conditions
must be fulfilled and letters rogatory presented.[69] No conflict between treaty and law was involved in either of these
cases. Furthermore, in another case it was held that letters
rogatory were not obligatory.[70]

On the other hand, there have been a number of cases
where the courts applied French laws, even though they
conflicted with earlier treaties:

On September 27, 1914 a decree was passed which declared

---

[67] S. 1888. 1. 17; *supra,* pp. 146.

[68] Pillet, *op. cit.,* p. 157.

[69] *Tribunal civil* of Nimes, Nov. 19, 1886; *Affaire Rebard*; Cl. 1889,
295; *Cour d'appel* of Paris, April 7, 1887; *Affaire Poss*; Cl. 1891, 533.

[70] *Tribunal civil* of Havre, Jan. 8, 1885; case of *Trombetta et Carrara
v. Compagnie les Deux-Pôles*; Cl. 1885, 293.

null and void every act or contract performed or entered into
in France proper or French protectorates with subjects of
Germany or Austria-Hungary, or persons residing in Germany or Austria-Hungary; all " commercial relations " with
such persons were forbidden by the decree. The execution
of pecuniary or other obligations resulting from any act or
contract done or entered into in France or French protectorates by any person with a German, prior to August 4,
1914, or with an Austro-Hungarian, prior to August 13,
1914, was also prohibited.[71]

In a number of cases the courts had to decide whether this
decree denied Germans and Austro-Hungarians access to the
French courts. The decision depended on the interpretation
given to the words " act or contract " and " execution " in
the decree. If among " acts and contracts " the engagement
of counsel were included, no German or Austro-Hungarian
could be represented in court. Furthermore, if the term
" execution " were stretched to include judicial settlement of
pecuniary or other obligations between French citizens and
Germans or Austro-Hungarians, the latter would in effect be
barred from French courts. As we shall see, this was the
interpretation which most French courts gave to the decree.[72]

This broad interpretation of the decree brought it into
conflict with article 23 h of the " Regulations " annexed to
the Fourth Hague Convention of 1907 (dealing with the
laws and customs of war on land), which had received the
approval of the Chambers and had been duly promulgated;

---

[71] Text in Cl. 1915, 105; text of the law of April 4, 1915 which prescribed penalties for infractions of this decree, *ibid.*, p. 108. The decree
was a so-called " *décret-loi* ", passed in execution of the law of Aug. 5,
1914 which authorized the government to suspend during hostilities the
effects of commercial and civil obligations with alien enemies. The
decree was, therefore, equivalent to a law as long as it did not exceed
the powers granted by the law of Aug. 5, 1914.

[72] See *infra*, pp. 154-155, 183-184.

article 23 h prohibited " to declare extinguished, suspended, or unenforceable in a court of law the rights and rights of action of the nationals of the adverse party ". The article was interpreted in continental Europe as guaranteeing the right of private alien enemies to have access to the courts during hostilities.[73]   Great Britain and the United States, however, maintained that the article referred solely to the rights of enemy nationals in occupied territories.[74]

The different meaning attributed to article 23 h in England and America, as compared to continental Europe, is due to the fundamental difference of view in Anglo-American as against continental European jurisprudence, regarding the status of enemy nationals not serving in the armed forces of the enemy.   For three generations before the World War the majority of continental European writers proclaimed that war was waged between states only and consequently no relation of enmity existed between the nationals of the belligerents, provided they did not serve in the armed forces, nor between one belligerent state and such nationals of the adverse party.[75]   This doctrine goes back to Rousseau[76] and was first proclaimed by the eminent French lawyer and statesman Portalis at the opening of the French prize court in 1801.[77]   The doctrine has never been accepted in Anglo-American jurisprudence.

[73] See *Deuxième conférence internationale de la paix, actes et documents*, vol. iii, p. 103; *Weissbuch über die Ergebnisse der im Jahre 1907 im Haag abgehaltenen Friedenskonferenz*; Politis, " *L'article 23 h du Règlement de la Haye* ", in RGDP. (1914), p. 249; Wehberg, *Capture in war on land and sea* (London, 1911), p. 8; Kohler in Z. V. (1911), p. 384; Strupp in Z. V. (1910), p. 56.

[74] See Oppenheim, *The League of Nations* (London, 1919), pp. 48-55.

[75] See Oppenheim, *International Law* (London, 1928), 4th ed., vol. ii, p. 118; Hall, *International Law* (Oxford, 1924), 8th ed., pp. 84-91.

[76] Rousseau, *Contrat Social*, vol. i, chapter iv.

[77] See Hall, *op. cit.*, p. 86; Lassudrie-Duchène, *Jean Jacques Rousseau et le droit des gens* (Paris, 1906).

The French courts declared that international law forbids belligerents to close their courts to alien enemies; they regarded article 23 h as declaratory of a rule of customary international law and cited it merely as an additional proof that alien enemies have access to the courts. Most of the cases dealing with the decree of 1914 are, therefore, discussed in the next chapter, which deals with the enforcement of customary international law by the French courts.[78] However, in one case, that of *Daude v. Johann Faber et Wilmoth, séquestre,*[79] the *Tribunal de la Seine,* through its *" référé ",* president Monier, discussed the conflict between the 1914 decree and article 23 h of the Hague Convention of 1907 and declared that the court was bound by the later French law.[80]

This was a suit instituted by the French creditor Daude against the German pencil manufacturer Faber and his sequestrator Wilmoth. President Monier, therefore, pro-

[78] See *infra,* pp. 180-186.

[79] The confiscated property of alien enemies was entrusted in France to so-called *administrateurs-séquestres* who were appointed by the courts in their common law jurisdiction, and who were subject to the control of the courts. The government occasionally issued regulations for the guidance of the courts.

These sequestrators were trustees who had to preserve the property, with a view to protect rights of French creditors and to prevent the property from aiding the enemy. The income was received by them and out of it French creditors were paid; the rest went to the *Caisse de Dépôts et Consignations* (a part of the public treasury). Except for the control exercised over them by the courts, the French sequestrators had functions and powers similar to the United States Alien Property Custodian; see Garner, *International Law during the World War* (London, 1920), vol. i, pp. 89-93, 104.

[80] The decree of Sept. 27, 1914 was a so-called *décret-loi,* passed in execution of the law of Aug. 5, 1914 which authorized the government to suspend during hostilities the effects of commercial and civil obligations with alien enemies. The conflict was, therefore, one between a treaty, approved by the legislature, and a decree authorized by a law and having force of law.

ceeded to examine whether a suit against an alien enemy was permitted in French law. He found that every suit involves " acts " and includes a " contract " with a lawyer, both in his opinion, forbidden by the decree of 1914. He interpreted the decree as prohibiting every act of alien enemies " which would constitute on their part a manifestation of their existence and of their legal personality ".[81] and especially the right of access to French courts.[82] In his opinion there existed no doubt that the decree withdrew the right of access to the courts from Germans and Austro-Hungarians. In view of this fact, he said:

We must reject the arguments drawn from the *speculative theories of the law of nations,* and especially from the positive right of " free access," consecrated for the Germans in France in the civil code and particularly in article 23 of the " Regulations " annexed to the Fourth Hague Convention of October 18, 1907. In the first place, *an international treaty cannot prevail against a later municipal law* which modifies its dispositions and which must be rigorously respected from the moment when it comes into force, by all persons living in [French] territory.[83]

Having laid down the principle that a treaty cannot prevail against a subsequent municipal law, he attempted to justify this law, first, by arguing that Germany had, prior to France, violated article 23 h of the Hague convention in question by the enactment of a decree of the Bundesrat of Aug. 7, 1914; second, by an accusation of Germany's methods of warfare,

[81] Cl. 1916, 1303, 1304.

[82] To support this interpretation of the decree, president Monier cited the report of the committee on commerce and industry of the Chamber of deputies, on the law of Jan. 19, 1915 which approved the decree of 1914; furthermore, the text of the law of April 4, 1915 which contains the punitive sanctions of the decree. His main emphasis, however, was on the " spirit " of the decree which, so he argued, did not permit a restrictive interpretation of the term " commercial relations ", which are the only relations which the decree forbids.

[83] Decision of May 18, 1916; Cl. 1916, 1303, 1306 (italics inserted).

which, in his opinion, had been conducted with such cruelty and inhuman excesses that Germany must be charged with having violated all the rules contained in the Hague conventions, and that, therefore: " one cannot think of according German nationals the benefits of the law of nations or of the treaties which Germany has violated at every opportunity ".[84]

The decision has been severely criticized by J. Barthélemy.[85] He pointed out that president Monier was misinformed on the German decree of Aug. 7, 1914 [86] which did not violate article 23 h of the Fourth Hague Convention, and ridiculed his argument that because of German excesses in Belgium and violation of the rules of land warfare, a German pencil manufacturer was denied the right to defend himself against the action instituted against him by one of his French creditors.[87]

[84] Cl. 1916, 1303, 1307.

[85] J. Barthélemy, "De l'accès des sujets ennemis aux tribunaux français", Cl. 1916, 1473.

[86] The German decree was a defense measure to protect German debtors; it prohibited suits by all persons residing outside Germany—regardless of nationality—against Germans, unless permission was obtained from the chancellor. This prohibition was limited to suits for the recovery of debts or patrimonial claims (vermögensrechtliche Ansprüche). Persons residing outside Germany could entertain actions relating to status, guardianship, etc.; they could be represented by counsel. In its decision of Oct. 26, 1914 (supra, pp. 37-39) the Reichsgericht entertained a suit by a Frenchman, domiciled in Paris, for the infringement of patent rights. Furthermore, the decree permitted alien enemies, residing in Germany, and enemy branch offices in Germany to sue. On the German practice, see: Garner, International Law and the World War, vol. i, pp. 144-46. Articles in Clunet by Dr. K. Hirschland, Cl. 1917, 87; W. Haber, Cl. 1917, 448; J. Barthélemy, Cl. 1916, 1473; A. Curti, Cl. 1915, 785.

[87] On May 23, 1916, by order of the court, the sequestrator of Faber was directed to sell merchandise, confiscated from Faber, and to pay Daude's claim therefrom. (Tribunal de la Seine, through "référé", president Monier, Cl. 1916, 1275). Barthélemy maintained that the action against Faber was in the nature of a revenge and could not be termed a reprisal, as it did not serve to induce the enemy to desist from his illegal practices.

The case was not appealed.   The point which interests us here is that the court felt bound by the later municipal law which it admitted to be in conflict with a previously concluded treaty.   The attempt made by president Monier to justify the decree as a reprisal for internationally illegal acts of Germany shows his desire to avoid a conflict between treaty and law.   This desire did not, however, influence his interpretation of the French law; he gave a very broad meaning to the decree and was unwilling to restrict it in order " to render inopportune respect to a treaty which the adverse party has, since the outbreak of hostilities—together with all other treaties of a similar character—cynically violated and trampled under foot ".[88]   We shall find the same attitude expressed in the decisions of a number of other French courts which will be cited in the next chapter, since they based the right of free access to the courts primarily on an alleged rule of customary international law.[89]

The relation between treaties and subsequent municipal laws modifying their provisions has been extensively discussed in connection with French war and post-war legislation for the benefit of tenants.[90]

The laws of March 7, 1918, April 1, 1926, and July 19, 1929—the last substantially restated the 1926 law as regards the sections which interest us here—stipulated that landlords could not terminate leases and evict their tenants.   This benefit of prorogation was denied to foreign tenants, with the exception of certain specified classes, such as subjects of protectorates, aliens whose children were French etc.   The 1926 law contained in article 4 a clause to the effect that the

[88] Cl. 1916, 1303, 1310.

[89] *Infra*, pp. 183-184.

[90] See Nogaro, *Les traités d'établissement et le droit des étrangers en France* (Paris, 1930) ; also articles by: Perroud in Cl. 1917, 295; Bartin in Cl. 1917, 17; Picard in Cl. 1926, 849.

exclusion of foreigners from the benefit of prorogation was to be understood as " reserving diplomatic treaties existing on the day of promulgation of this law ".

The treaties with Denmark of 1910, with Switzerland of 1882, and with the United States of 1853 contain provisions which substantially assimilate the nationals of one contracting state to those of the other, with respect to movable and immovable property. Many states could invoke these treaties by reason of most favoured nation clauses. There were, consequently, many litigations in which foreigners pleaded that the housing laws could not exclude them, as they were entitled to national treatment by reason of diplomatic treaties. The *Tribunal de la Seine* took three different views on this question:

In *Magnam v. Schaad*[91] and *Panton v. Eyre*[92] it argued that article 4 of the 1926 law granted the privilege of prorogation to foreigners who could invoke treaties granting them national treatment, but that, since this was a matter of civil rights, article 11 of the civil code must be complied with, which states: " The foreigner enjoys in France the same civil rights which are accorded to Frenchmen by treaty in the country whose subject he is ". The court implied that the civil code had not been superseded by the treaties granting foreigners national treatment[93] and demanded proof of reciprocity by treaty from the foreign tenant who desired to benefit from the housing laws. In the two cases cited, it found that no such reciprocity existed between France and the states to which the foreign tenants belonged; consequently the benefits of the housing laws were denied to them.

[91] Decision of June 28, 1926; Cl. 1927, 415.

[92] Decision of Jan. 26, 1927; Dall. hebd., 1927, p. 232.

[93] No distinction was drawn between the treaties with Switzerland of 1882 and with Denmark of 1910, which had received legislative approval, and the treaty with the United States of 1853 which had not.

In *Nacos v. Martin* [94] and *Beltran-Masses v. Guibert* [95] the court did not insist on reciprocity by treaty, but was satisfied with reciprocity in fact. It found that Spain and Greece had similar housing laws from which Frenchmen benefited there, and accorded the same rights to the two foreign tenants.

In *Schramek v. Bruder,* [96] *Micheline v. Fischer* [97] and *Chevallier v. Thomas* [98] the court held that although this was a matter of civil rights, article 11 of the civil code had been overruled by the treaties with Switzerland of 1882 and with Spain of 1862, and that therefore, the foreign tenants benefited by the law of 1926. [99]

The *Cour de cassation* [100] took the first view and the lower courts quickly followed. It argued that the treaties had not been intended to refer to this special war legislation, and that, furthermore, this being a matter of civil rights, it was necessary that the foreigner, who desired to avail himself of the privilege of prorogation, show that in his country Frenchmen were given reciprocal rights by treaty, in accordance with the requirements of article 11 of the civil code. [101]

[94] Decision of July 25, 1927; Cl. 1928, 976.

[95] Decision of Dec. 26, 1927; Cl. 1928, 1006. This decision was reversed by the *Cour de cassation* on June 23, 1928; Cl. 1929, 90.

[96] Decision of July 28, 1925; G. P. 1926. 2. 705.

[97] Decision of March 8, 1927; Dall. hebd. 1927, p. 343; the decision was reversed by the *Cour de cassation* on Aug. 1, 1927; G. P. 1927. 2. 635.

[98] Decision of March 7, 1927; Dall. hebd. 1927, p. 344.

[99] In the same sense: *Justice de paix* of Dijon, July 9, 1926; *Blaise v. Burnier*; G. P. of Oct. 3, 1926; reversed by the *Cour de cassation,* May 30, 1927; Cl. 1928, 398.

[100] A special commission (*Commission supérieure*) was formed in the *Cour de cassation* to deal with cases arising under the tenant laws.

[101] *Blaise v. Burnier,* May 30, 1927; Cl. 1928, 398; *Micheline v. Fischer,* Aug. 1, 1927; G. P. 1927. 2. 635; *Beltran-Masses v. Guibert,* June 23, 1928, Cl. 1929, 90; *Bazie v. Dlle-Weatherby,* May 30, 1927, Cl. 1928, 400; *Fitz-Gerald v. de Villeneuve,* June 13, 1927; Cl. 1928, 403; *Spalding de*

Since the law of 1926 had expressly reserved treaties, it could not be regarded as conflicting with any prior treaty. The cases are, however, cited as their narrow interpretation of the treaties granting national treatment to the citizens of the contracting parties was followed in a number of cases where a conflict existed between treaties and subsequent French laws.

Article 5 of the law of 1926 stipulated that whenever the proprietor or members of his family wished to occupy his premises, he could evict the tenant; the latter could not avail himself in such cases of the right of prorogation. Only French proprietors were granted this so-called " *droit de reprise* "; foreign proprietors were barred from this privilege and there was no saving clause reserving treaty rights. The courts argued that *qui dicit de uno negat de altero,* in other words, that omission of the treaty clause in article 5 of the 1926 law meant that the legislator did not intend to make any exceptions in favor of foreigners who could invoke treaties.

While the right of prorogation constituted a special favor to the tenant which might conceivably be reserved to Frenchmen in spite of treaties granting foreigners national treatment in the enjoyment of movable and immovable property, the *droit de reprise* on the other hand, constituted a restitution of part of the common law rights of property which had been taken away from landlords by this special war legislation. It is evidently incorrect to compare the *droit de reprise* with the *droit de prorogation* and to maintain that both are special rights to which the treaties did not refer. However, this was the view taken by the *Cour de cassation.* It was followed by the lower courts.

Garmondia v. Cochard, Jan. 6, 1928; G. P. 1928. 2. 66; *Figone v. Gonder,* June 29, 1929; G. P. Oct. 10, 1929; *Nobili v. Houssard,* March 1, 1928; G. P. 1928. 2. 67.

The *Tribunal de la Seine* rendered two interesting decisions dealing with the *droit de reprise*. In *Chenouard v. Denis* it argued that the treaty with the United States of 1853 did not regulate the manner in which property could be enjoyed; it merely assimilated Americans to Frenchmen as regards the acquisition and transmission of property. This was a curious argument, as the treaty obviously intended to give Americans the same rights of property enjoyed by Frenchmen, and not merely the doubtful right to acquire property whose uses could by law be completely taken away from them, because of their foreign nationality. After this feeble attempt to reconcile treaty and law, the court said:

Even if it were true that the treaty of 1853 regulated the manner in which property rights may be enjoyed, it would be abrogated by the precise terms of article 5 of the subsequent law of 1926. *It is not the judge's province to inquire whether the legislator of 1926 had, according to international law, the legislative competence required for the validity of the statute as regards the law of nations; being an internal organ, the court must judge the statute according to the criteria of municipal law only.*[102]

In *Rockwell v. Leroy* the same court made no attempt to harmonize treaty and law, but accepted the conflict and applied the later French law, saying:

If the French judge would accord to the American proprietor the same right to oppose prorogation as it is possessed by the French proprietor, contrary to the clear text of article 5 [of the law of 1926], he would disregard *the hierarchy of the treaty and the law;* he would transgress the internal law and overstep the rights of the judicial power. *He must,* on the contrary, *follow the will of the legislator which is imposed upon him.*[103]

[102] Decision of Oct. 27, 1926; Cl. 1927, 420 (italics inserted).

[103] Decision of Nov. 22, 1926; G. P. 1927. I. 96 (italics inserted). In the same sense see: *Dussaud v. Losching, Tribunal de la Seine,* Dec. 28, 1928; G. P. of Dec. 28, 1928; *Fransioli v. Alcalay,* Cl. 1928, 391 (same

The *Cour de cassation* did not admit a conflict between article 5 of the law of 1926 and treaties, but repeated its arguments in the matter of prorogation. As it found that in none of the cases which came before it, the *droit de reprise* was expressly granted to Frenchmen by treaty in the states whose nationals sought to avail themselves of this right, it denied the *droit de reprise* to them.[104]

Finally the laws of June 30, 1926 and April 22, 1927 should be mentioned, which stipulated for rights of prorogation of tenants of industrial property. The first law excluded certain classes of foreigners, the second excluded all foreigners; neither mentioned treaties.

In two cases the *Tribunal de la Seine* held that the treaties with Spain of 1862, with Greece of 1924 and with Denmark of 1910 must be applied, as the laws did not intend to violate rights granted to foreigners therein. In *Lucas-Moreno v. Banque commerciale africaine* it said: "The treaties and conventions which are in force today protect the citizens of the states with which they have been concluded; a municipal law could, therefore, not brusquely modify their effects."[105]

In *Betsou v. Volzenlogel* it decided that by reason of the most favored nation clause in the treaty with Greece of 1924, the treaty with Denmark of 1910 which provided for national treatment in property rights applied. As regards the law of 1926 it said:

court), decision of Apr. 4, 1927. Both cases dealt with the treaty with Switzerland of 1882. For a minority decision, holding that the law did not intend to violate the treaty with Switzerland of 1882, see: *Tribunal civil of Colmar*, in *Weyl-Block v. Bigler*, Feb. 20, 1929, Cl. 1930, 127.

[104] The Franco-Swiss treaty of 1882 and the Franco-Spanish treaty of 1862 were invoked; the court made no distinction between the former which had received legislative approval and the latter which had not. See *Pigasson v. Kuhn*, Aug. 1, 1927, G. P. 1927. 2. 636; *Pelayo v. Lecaux*, Aug. 1, 1927, G. P. 1927. 2. 635; *Antolin v. Concure*, Oct. 25, 1928, G. P. of Nov. 17, 1928.

[105] Decision of Dec. 12, 1927; Cl. 1928, 982.

The law of June 30, 1926 cannot have the effect of depriving Danish subjects of an advantage which is assured them by a diplomatic treaty. . . . A treaty between states is, like a contract between individuals, a reciprocal engagement which must be respected by both parties until the treaty is denounced or superseded by a new treaty.[106]

However, after the decision of the *Cour d'appel* of Paris on July 2, 1928, in *Spilka v. Lerche*,[107] in which the usual arguments regarding the necessity of treaty reciprocity, as set forth by the *Cour de cassation* on numerous occasions, were repeated, and the law of 1926 applied, the *Tribunal de la Seine* reversed itself and followed the court of appeal.[108]

The courts were thus, finally, all lined up in favor of the later municipal law. The *Cour de cassation,* and following it, the lower courts refused to admit a conflict between treaty and subsequent law, but their interpretation of the treaties was manifestly incorrect.[109]

The French foreign office received numerous protests and on July 20, 1929 an exchange of letters took place between the British ambassador and the French minister of foreign affairs,[110] in which it was agreed that British subjects could invoke treaties in which national treatment was granted—by reason of the most favored nation clause—, and that these treaties had not been abrogated by the tenant laws. On July 22, 1929 the minister of foreign affairs addressed a letter to

[106] Decision of Dec. 23, 1927; Cl. 1928, 998.

[107] G. P. 1928. 2. 323.

[108] *Proost v. Berger*, G. P. of Feb. 2, 1929; *Cavanagh v. Bestegui*, G. P. 1929. 1. 826.

[109] In *Bazie v. Dlle-Weatherby*, Cl. 1928, 400, the *Cour de cassation* made the flagrant mistake of stating that the Anglo-French treaty of 1882 dealt only with commercial and maritime matters. The preamble of the treaty declared that the treaty was destined " *à régler l'état des relations commerciales et maritimes entre les deux pays, ainsi que l'établissement de leurs nationaux* ".

[110] *Journal officiel*, July 20, 1929.

the *Garde des sceaux* which he, in turn, transmitted to the *procureurs généraux*.[111] In this letter the minister of foreign affairs asserted his " constitutional right " to correct the misinterpretation of treaties by the courts when thereby conflicts have been caused with foreign states. He declared that the treaties granting national treatment to the subjects of the contracting state remained in force despite the tenant laws, and that the latter must be understood to exclude only those foreigners who could not invoke such treaties. A list of the relevant treaties was annexed to the letter.

The *Cour de cassation* accepted this interpretation and forthwith applied and interpreted treaties in accordance with the letter of the minister of foreign affairs, transmitted to the court through the *Garde de sceaux*.[112]

In conclusion we may say that where treaties conflict with subsequent French laws, the courts will apply the later law; they are inclined to endeavor to establish an apparent harmony of treaty and law, by interpreting the former strictly. The *Tribunal de la Seine* has at times acknowledged a conflict and applied the later law,[113] but the *Cour de cassation* has never admitted the existence of a conflict between treaty and law and has regularly applied the later law.[114]

[111] *Journal officiel* of Aug. 13, 1929. The *Garde des sceaux* heads the ministry of justice; the *procureurs généraux* are attorneys-general.

[112] *Laudelle v. Cavaille*, G. P. Nov. 28, 1929; *Guldenschu v. Pigeard*, G. P. Jan. 5, 1930; see Nogaro, *op. cit.*, p. 139. Curiously enough, the courts of appeal refused to comply with the interpretation of the treaties by the minister of foreign affairs; see Nogaro, *op. cit.*, p. 140. The whole question is discussed by Scheurer in *Zeitschrift für ausländisches öffentliches Recht und Völkerrecht* (1930), vol. ii, pp. 112, 114-121.

[113] *Daude v. Wilmoth*; Cl. 1916, 1303; S. 1920. 2. 20; *Chenouard v. Denis*, Cl. 1929, 420; *Rockwell v. Leroy*, G. P. 1927. 1. 96. On the other hand, the same court has in two decisions interpreted the law of June 30, 1926, as not intending to violate treaty rights: *Lucas-Moreno v. Banque commerciale africaine*, Cl. 1928, 982; *Betsou v. Volzenlogel*, G. P. 1928. 1. 97. It has, however, reversed itself later on, see *supra*, p. 162.

[114] The chief criticism against the interpretation of treaties in these cases

The *Cour de cassation* will, upon instructions from the minister of foreign affairs, transmitted to it through the *Garde des sceaux,* reverse its interpretation of a treaty and accept his interpretation.[115]

The cases cited show a marked tendency on the part of the French courts to interpret treaties in the same manner as laws, viz. by supplementing and clarifying ambiguous terms through recourse to French laws. This lack of respect for the intention of the other contracting state is ex-

by the *Cour de cassation* (and the lower courts), is its insistence that all treaties must be interpreted so as to conform to article 11 of the civil code. This seems to indicate an unwillingness on its part to admit that a later treaty can abrogate the civil code, a principle, which, at least where the treaty has received legislative approval, has been maintained in a number of cases (see *supra*, pp. 138-140). In the tenant cases the courts did not distinguish between the effects of the treaties with Switzerland of 1882 and Denmark of 1910—approved by the Chambers—as against that with the United States of 1853, concluded under the 1852 constitution by the emperor alone.

French courts show great firmness in upholding the principle that municipal laws cannot abrogate treaties when it is not a question of their own laws. In *Stern v. Procureur de la Republique* the *Tribunal de la Seine* said, with regard to the treaty between Prussia and the United States of 1868 (Bancroft treaty) and the nationality laws of the German Empire: "To hold that the imperial constitution of 1871 terminated the treaty of 1868, except in so far as its provisions have been carried over into the nationality laws of the Empire, one would have to admit that a diplomatic treaty can be modified by the dispositions of an internal law of one of the contracting states. Such a conception is directly contrary to the most definite rules of international law and is wholly inacceptable." (Cl. 1918, 238). Rejecting the "abnormal German doctrine" (reference is made to the Laband-Gneist doctrine), the court applied the treaty to the case (decision of July 17, 1917). The opposition of French writers and judges against the German dualistic theory seems strange, in view of the fact that it is so thoroughly in accord with the practice of French courts.

[115] As to the consequences of a wrong interpretation of a treaty by the minister of foreign affairs, see the interesting arbitral decision of the Swiss arbiter Ador between France and Spain, rendered Jan. 15, 1922. (Printed by Valéry in "*L'Impôt sur les bénéfices de guerre et les commerçants espagnols*", Cl. 1923, 223).

plained by Bartin as being due to the fact that the courts apply treaties as laws.[116] Even where the courts profess to inquire into the intention of the contracting states, as e. g. in the *Duke of Richmond* case, they evidently consider only the intentions of the French negotiators who " could not have intended" the treaty to be in opposition " to all the rules of French civil and public law ".[117]

From the point of view of international law, this practice is most unsatisfactory and apt to occasion diplomatic protests.[118] The difficulty is to a great extent obviated by a principle enunciated and consistently applied by the *Cour de cassation* and, with some fluctuations, by the lower courts, viz. that treaties can be interpreted by judicial courts only in suits involving private interests; whenever public interests are at stake, the courts must ask the government for its interpretation of the treaty. This principle was first an-

[116] Bartin, *Principes de droit international privé* (Paris, 1930), p. 105; he cites several cases where the courts interpreted treaties with ambiguous terms by supplementing them with French laws; The Franco-Swiss treaty of 1828, which regulated the succession of the nationals of one country in the other country, was supplemented by the French law of 1819 and the provisions of the treaty thereby interpreted in a manner advantageous to French heirs (*Cour de cassation*, July 18, 1859, D. 1859. 1. 325) ; similarly the *Cour d'appel* of Amiens restricted the meaning of the treaty with Austria of 1866 by supplementing it with the law of 1819 (Nov. 26, 1891, D. 1892.2.428). The treaty with Spain of 1862 exempted nationals of one state born on the territory of the other from military service there. Its terms were not clear as to whether a person born in France of a Spanish father who himself had been born in France was included in this exemption. The *Cour d'appel* of Bordeau (Dec. 21, 1892, Cl. 1893, 565; July 11, 1892, Cl. 1892, 937) supplemented the treaty with the French nationality laws of 1851 and 1874, and decided that such persons were not included in the treaty exemption. In none of these cases did the courts examine the intentions of the negotiators which, in the opinion of Bartin, had been evidently contrary to the interpretation which the French courts gave to the treaties.

[117] S. 1839. 1. 577; see *supra*, pp. 140-141.

[118] See the protests against the decisions of the courts in the tenant cases, *supra*, pp. 162-163.

nounced by the *Cour de cassation* in the *Duke of Richmond* case [119] and has been restated again and again.[120] The reasons for this principle have been very clearly stated by the *Tribunal de la Seine* in *Chancelier de l'ambassade d'Italie à Paris v. Desouches:*

Diplomatic treaties are not administrative acts but have, as soon as they are duly promulgated, the character of laws in regard to the nationals of the two states who have concluded the treaty, and the character of contracts in regard to the contracting states themselves. Their interpretation by judicial courts [121] depends on the nature of the dispute brought before them, and of the persons between whom it has arisen; judicial courts are authorized to interpret them when they relate to private interests which are, by the law of nations, within their competence; . . . on the other hand, all questions which interest the *ordre public* [122] are not within their competence. In the latter case, their decision might constitute an infraction of the *imperium* of the state with whom the treaty was concluded and might influence the relations of the two states; the treaty can, therefore, be interpreted by the contracting states themselves only.[123]

The court emphasized the fact that treaties are not administrative acts, because the law of 16 *fruct. an* III forbids judicial courts to take cognizance of administrative acts.[124]

[119] S. 1839. 1. 577.

[120] See, for instance: *Cour de cassation,* Aug. 11, 1841. S. 1841. 1. 848; Jan. 6, 1873, Cl. 1874, 245; July 27, 1877, Cl. 1878, 166; June 30, 1884, Cl. 1885, 306. See also the cases cited by Appert: "*De l'interpretation des traités diplomatiques au cours d'un procès*"; Cl. 1899, 433, and the anonymous article in Cl. 1913, 23.

[121] The court wishes to distinguish judicial from administrative courts.

[122] The phrase *ordre public* cannot be adequately depicted by any English term. It includes such conceptions as "public order", "public safety" and "public policy". On the meaning of *ordre public* consult: Pillet et Niboyet, *Manuel de droit international privé* (Paris, 1924), pp. 406-422.

[123] Decision of April 11, 1900; Cl. 1900, 624.

[124] Gradually this principle has been modified and today the judicial

These are withdrawn from the competence of the judicial courts and assigned to a special administrative court, the *Conseil d'État*.

Inasmuch as the *Conseil d'État* has taken the position that it can apply a treaty, but that it can never interpret it, the interpretation being exclusively a right of the government, it is necessary for an understanding of the different practice of the *Conseil d'État* and the judicial courts, to state briefly certain principles of French administrative law.

As a result of the principle of the separation of powers, the revolutionary constitutions established the complete independence of the administration from the courts.[125] To safeguard private rights, the laws of March 3, 1849 and May 24, 1872 gave the *Conseil d'État* jurisdiction over suits against the administration.[126] The jurisdiction of the

courts may interpret administrative acts relating to the public domain, unless they have been withdrawn from them and transferred to the *Conseil d'État* by a special law. See Berthélemy: *Traité de droit administratif,* 11th ed. (Paris, 1926), p. 25.

The *Conseil d'État*, established by the constitution of 22 *frim. an* VIII, is the successor of the *Conseil du roi* which existed since the reign of Henry III. Since 1849 it acts as an administrative tribunal in addition to its legislative and administrative functions. The law of July 13, 1879 fixed the membershp of the *Conseil d'État* at 99, including the minister of justice, the president and the secretary-general.

[125] Law of Aug. 16-24, 1790, title ii, art. 13. See Laferrière, *Traité de juridiction administrative* (Paris, 1896), 2nd ed., vol. i, p. 477.

[126] Previously the *Conseil d'État* had heard protests against administrative acts, but it had done so as an organ of the administration, and not as a court. Since 1849, it has been a regular administrative tribunal. (In 1872 there was created a *Tribunal des conflits* to decide conflicts of competence between the judicial courts and the *Conseil d'État*). Administrative acts are divided into two classes according to French administrative law: first, acts *jure gestionis*, viz. acts of the government performed for the profit of the public domain and the functioning of the public services, resembling acts of individuals in the management of their affairs; second, acts *jure imperii*, viz. acts performed by the government in its sovereign capacity, such as orders issued by it to its subjects, commanding them to do or to refrain from doing certain acts. (Laferrière, *op. cit.*, vol. i,

Conseil d'État is clearly defined by law and refers only to suits against the administration in regard to *administrative* acts. French constitutional law, however, regards certain acts of the executive as so-called *actes de gouvernement* and distinguishes them from administrative acts. These *actes de gouvernement* emanate from the political power of the executive which is distinct from his administrative power.[127] Since the competence of the *Conseil d'État* is, by the law of May 24, 1872, limited to administrative acts, it has no jurisdiction over *actes de gouvernement*.[128] [129]   Treaties are re-

pp. 13-15). The *Conseil d'État* decides suits against the state for acts *jure gestionis* in *actions de pleine juridiction* in exactly the same manner as courts decide litigations between two private individuals; the state is made the defendant. Acts *jure imperii* may be annulled by the *Conseil d'État* in *actions d'annullment* which are directed, not against the state, but against the act objectively. The *Conseil d'État* may not substitute its own decision in *actions d'annullment*, but must limit itself to an annullment of the act. The power given to the *Conseil d'État* to annul acts of the state *jure imperii* is a distinct creation of French administrative law.

[127] Laferrière analyzes administrative and governmental powers as follows: "To administer means to assure the daily application of the law, to watch over the relations of the citizens with the central and local administrations and between the various administrations themselves. To govern means to watch over the observation of the constitution, the functioning of the great public powers, to guarantee the relations of the government with the Chambers and those of the state with foreign powers"; *op. cit.*, vol. ii, p. 33.

[128] The theory is that although such acts might violate private rights, the government is authorized to do so where this is necessary for the social good or the national defense, and in that case the government is responsible to the legislature only and not to the courts. The *actes de gouvernement* theory has been criticized by the following French writers: Michoud, "*Des Actes de gouvernement*", *Revue de l'Université de Grenoble* (1889), p. 263; Brémond, "*Des Actes de gouvernement*", *Revue du droit public* (1890), vol. i, p. 23; Berthélemy, *Traité élémentaire de droit administratif*, 11th ed. (Paris, 1926), p. 137. They claim that the *actes de gouvernement* are really administrative acts, but that their nature is such that they cannot be disputed by individuals before the courts; the courts not being the arbiter

garded by the *Conseil d'État* as *actes de gouvernement* and it is for this reason that it refuses to interpret them.

The position taken by the *Conseil d'État* is strictly correct. Even if it were argued that treaties became laws by virtue of the approval of the legislature and promulgation, and that in municipal law they must be assimilated to laws, the *Conseil d'État* would be incompetent to interpret them. As Dalloz says in his *Répertoire:*

In accordance with the text of article 9 of the law of 1872 . . . the *Conseil d'État* may not take cognizance of acts which are not administrative acts; the following are therefore withdrawn from its supervision: 1. Acts having the character of laws or made in pursuance of a delegation of power by the legislature. . . .[130]

Both in their character as international contracts, and as municipal laws, treaties may not be interpreted by the *Conseil d'État*. The incompetence of the *Conseil d'État* is due solely to the fact that French administrative law has not extended its jurisdiction to this field.

between the government and the legislature. This theory reaches the same practical results as the older one which regards certain acts as *actes de gouvernement*. Duguit, *Manuel de droit constitutionnel* (Paris, 1923), p. 117, would class such treaties separately from administrative acts, although he regards them as being inherently administrative acts. The difficulty confronting French jurists is the action of the legislature in approving treaties, viz. whether they vote for the treaty as assistants to the administrative or executive power, or as a legislature only? In other words, is their approval an administrative or a legislative act? In view of the constant assertion of the judicial courts that treaties duly promulgated, which have received legislative approval, are laws, it would seem that the approval of the legislature is a legislative act. The whole question is rendered rather complicated by the French theory of the separation of powers.

[129] *The Conseil d'État* has constantly enlarged its jurisdiction and regards today many acts as administrative acts which it formerly treated as *actes de gouvernement*. Treaties are among the few acts which the *Conseil d'État* still regards as *actes de gouvernement*.

[130] Dalloz, *Répertoire*, under "*Conseil d'État*", no. 238.

The position of the judicial courts is entirely different. Having once established that treaties have within France the force of laws and are not administrative acts, they have in French law competence to interpret them. The reason why they ask for an interpretation by the government, in cases where a treaty deals with questions of international law, is their desire to avoid diplomatic controversies. Being conscious of the double nature of a treaty, viz. its character as a contract in international law and as a statute in municipal law, the courts have found that their doctrine is the best compromise. Considerations akin to the " political question " doctrine and the " act of state " doctrine in Anglo-American jurisprudence may have played their part.[131]

The courts have found it difficult to draw a line between private and public interests, which they could consistently follow. The tendency has been to stretch private interests and to interpret public interests primarily in the sense of political interests, interests which might cause diplomatic controversies.

The courts have interpreted treaties in cases where the two parties were French or the two foreign, the foreign government not being interested since it was not a question affecting its *imperium*.[132] Cases where one party was under the jurisdiction of the co-signatory state, but without that state's *imperium* being affected, such as cases dealing with treaties on literary, artistic or industrial property,[133] and cases

---

[131] Compare : Kingsbury, " The act of state doctrine ", *American Journal of International Law*, vol. iv, p. 359; Dickinson, " International political questions in the national courts ", *ibid.*, vol. xix, p. 157; Field," Doctrine of political questions in the federal courts ", *Minnesota Law Review*, vol. viii, p. 485.

[132] For instance : Successions debated by heirs of the same nationality, see *Cour de cassation*, June 24, 1839; S. 1839. 1. 577; Aug. 11, 1841; S. 1841. 1. 848.

[133] *Cour de cassation*, March 19, 1869, Pataille, 1870, 179; April 7, 1869,

where the foreign government was only indirectly interested, because its nationals were affected, such as cases where the nationality of litigants was determined through application of a treaty.[134] The courts have even determined the extent of protectorates established by treaties where the suit dealt with private interests only.[135] The criterium is the nature of the suit and not of the treaty.[136] The same treaty may contain provisions which the courts will interpret and other which they will not interpret.[137]

The courts have suspended action and asked for an interpretation of the treaty by the government in cases dealing with extradition treaties,[138] consular treaties,[139] treaties stipulating for the protection of aliens.[140] cases of a political

Pataille, 1870, 315; May 27, 1870, Pataille, 1870, 188; *Tribunal de la Seine,* Dec. 5, 1884, Pataille, 1885, 152; *Cour d'appel* of Paris, May 18, 1892, Cl. 1892, 1164; *Cour d'appel* of Nimes, Dec. 2, 1893, Cl. 1894, 147.

[134] *Cour d'appel* of Bordeau, Dec. 21, 1892, Cl. 1893, 565; *Cour d'appel* of Bordeau, July 11, 1892, Cl. 1892, 937; *Cour de cassation,* March 6, 1877, Cl. 1877, 354; Nov. 23, 1881, Cl. 1883, 58.

[135] *Cour de cassation,* June 2, 1892, Cl. 1893, 836; S. 1893. 1. 160; Oct. 27, 1893, Cl. 1894, 349.

[136] Bartin, *op. cit.,* p. 103.

[137] The Treaty of Peace of 1814 contained many purely political clauses, but those invoked in the Duke of Richmond case were interpreted by the *Cour de cassation,* since the suit was of a private nature. The *Cour de cassation* refused to interpret the Treaty of Versailles in a case where it was claimed that the treaty had been violated by the Ruhr invasion (a suit by Thyssen); March 22, 1923, Cl. 1923, 847; see also decision of same court, Aug. 9, 1923, Cl. 1924, 396 to the same sense. The *Cour de cassation* interpreted, on the other hand, those sections of the Treaty of Versailles which dealt with the settlement of private debts, incurred before the war, by nationals of France and Germany. See decisions cited in RGDP. (1921), p. 463; see also Cl. 1923, 963.

[138] *Cour de cassation,* July 18, 1852, S. 1852. 1. 157; Dec. 23, 1852, S. 1853. 1. 400; Jan. 11, 1884, Cl. 1885, 80.

[139] *Cour de cassation,* July 24, 1861, D. 1861. 1. 342; June 30, 1884, Cl. 1885, 306; Feb. 23, 1912, Cl. 1913, 182; April 5, 1927, Cl. 1928, 142; *Cour d'appel* of Aix, Feb. 7, 1922, Cl. 1924, 157.

[140] *Cour de cassation,* July 27, 1877; S. 1877. 1. 485.

nature,[141] and recently, it appears, also cases dealing with treaties of protectorate.[142]   The courts have often stretched "application" of treaties to such an extent as to actually amount to interpretation;[143] this has been done especially with extradition treaties.[144]

The *Conseil d'État* has consistently refused to interpret treaties.[145]

French writers have found it difficult to explain the different practice of the judicial courts and the *Conseil d'État* in the matter of treaty interpretation.   It is important to understand that the *Conseil d'État* is actuated solely by considerations of French administrative law, while the judicial courts wish to avoid international complications through misinterpretation of treaties.   The principle developed by the judicial courts is very acceptable from the point of view of international law.   Its value would be greatly enhanced if the courts could devise a satisfactory method to meet the practical difficulties in its application.

Treaties are terminated, both in international law, and in municipal law, through action of the president of the Republic.   So held by the *Cour d'appel* of Paris in *Société*

[141] *Cour de cassation*, March 22, 1923, Cl. 1923, 847; Aug. 9, 1923, Cl. 1924, 396.

[142] *Cour de cassation*, June 2, 1923; D. 1923. 1. 217.

[143] *Cour de cassation*, March 6, 1877; S. 1879. 1. 305; Dec. 22, 1913; S. 1914. 1. 233; *Cour d'appel* of Hanoi, Nov. 17, 1897; S. 1899. 2. 17.

[144] *Cour de cassation*, April 26, 1900, D. 1900. 1. 366; Feb. 27, 1908, S. 1912. 1. 69.

[145] July 23, 1823; Rec. Lebon, 1823, 544; Nov. 22, 1826, Rec. Lebon, 1826, 717; Aug. 22, 1844, Rec. Lebon, 1844, 508; Nov. 18, 1869, Rec. Lebon, 1869, 891 ; Nov. 14, 1884, Cl. 1886, 592; see also Appert, " *De l'interpretation des traités diplomatiques au cours d'un procès*", Cl. 1899, 433; Prudhomme, *La loi territoriale et les traités diplomatiques* (Paris, 1910), ch. i; Bartin, *Principes de droit international privé* (Paris, 1930), pp. 98 *et seq.*; Anonymous article, " *De la limitation des cas dans lesquels les tribunaux judiciaires ou administratifs peuvent interpreter les conventions internationales* ", Cl. 1913, 23.

des usines Renault v. Société Rousski Renault. Applicants had asked that the defendant, a Russian company, pay security for costs. The latter replied that the Hague conventions of July 15-27, 1896, and July 17, 1905, which stipulated that nationals of one signatory state should not be required to give security for costs in the courts of another signatory state, applied to the case, as both France and Russia had signed the Hague conventions. The Russian company argued that the Hague conventions formed an " integral part of French municipal law " and could only be abrogated by a new law and not by a declaration of the president. When France recognized Russia *de jure,* the president had through the minister of foreign affairs notified the Soviet government that " until the successful conclusion of negotiations about to be undertaken, the treaties, conventions and agreements between France or her citizens and Russia will have no effect ". The following day Russia had acknowledged the receipt of this communication and negotiations for new treaties had been opened.

The court held that the president " has the power . . . to the exclusion of the legislature . . . to denounce treaties and terminate them or to merely suspend their effects if the interest of the country so warrants." [146]

---

[146] Decision of Jan. 28, 1926; Cl. 1926, 671. According to this case, a treaty, approved by the Chambers and consequently having force of law, can be terminated by an act of the president, i. e. by a mere decree. The court rests this decision on the argument that the law of approval is required solely to render certain treaties executory in France. It does not take into account the double character of treaties, although at other times French courts, as we have seen, have refused to apply a treaty admittedly valid in international law, because it had, in its character as a municipal law been abrogated by a subsequent French statute (*supra*, pp. 154, 160). The position of the German *Reichsgericht* in its decision of Oct. 26, 1914 (RGZ 85, 375) seems to be more logical (see *supra*, pp. 37-39).

CHAPTER III

Customary International Law

Cases involving questions of customary international law have frequently come before French courts. The courts have not hesitated to apply such rules, but they have seldom indicated why customary international law is obligatory on them. The relation between customary international law and French law, and the position of the former in French courts have never been fully discussed by any French court.

A few cases will be cited to show the willingness of the courts to apply rules of customary international law:

In the *Affaire Pappenheim* the *Cour royale* of Paris declared itself incompetent to entertain a suit against the minister of the Grand-Duke of Hesse, stating that the latter " enjoys the immunities granted to ministers of foreign powers by international law ".[1]

In *Dientz v. de la Jara* the *Tribunal civil de la Seine* discussed the immunity enjoyed by diplomatic representatives as follows:

Diplomatic representatives . . . have always been considered exempt from the jurisdiction of the state to which they are accredited. . . . Sanctioned[2] by the law of nations, this immunity must be respected by the courts as a rule *d'ordre public supérieur*[3] which they must follow and which dominates all the prescriptions of private law: *In France it has always been acknowledged and followed.* Although it has not been entered

[1] Decision of Aug. 21, 1841 ; S. 1841. 2. 592.

[2] The French word used here is *consacrée*.

[3] See *supra*, p. 166, note 122.

into our civil code, the debates on the civil code, nevertheless, show clearly that it was present in the minds of the editors of the code, and that they intended to maintain it, even though they did not embody it in a written rule of law. . . .[4]

The case *Ministère public v. L'équipage et les passagers du Carlo Alberto* was appealed to the *Cour de cassation* primarily on the grounds that the lower court had misinterpreted a rule of customary international law. The facts of the case were the following:

The Duchess de Berry had formed a conspiracy in Sardinia against Louis-Philippe of France. The conspirators sought to cause disturbances in Marseille and southern France. In the course of their attempt to win popular support there, some members of the conspiracy, who had chartered the Sardinian ship " Carlo Alberto ", were forced into the French port of Ciotat by distress. They were arrested by the French authorities. Alleging that, according to a generally recognized rule of customary international law, ships driven into a foreign port through distress were immune from the jurisdiction of the state to which the port belonged, the conspirators brought suit to have the writ of arrest vacated.

The *Cour royale* of Aix declared the arrest illegal, because in violation of the law of nations, and ordered the conspirators released. The court said:

The vessel " Carlo Alberto " is a Sardinian ship . . . it was forced into port through distress . . . such cases are among civilized states placed under the protection of good faith, humanity and generosity. . . . The arrests constitute, therefore, *a violation of the law of nations and of the generosity which the French nation has always practiced* . . . they [the arrests] must consequently be considered null and void, and the persons arrested must be released and conducted to Sardinian territory.[5]

[4] Decision of July 31, 1878; Cl. 1878, 500 (italics inserted).
[5] Decision of Aug. 6, 1832; cited in S. 1832. 1. 578 (italics inserted).

The attorney-general appealed to the *Cour de cassation* from this decision. Citing many cases, he maintained that the rule of customary international law according to which ships driven into port by distress are immune from the jurisdiction of the state to which the port belongs, was inapplicable in a case where persons on board a ship had been guilty of hostile acts against that state. The *Cour de cassation* reversed the decision of the lower court, stating that:

The privilege accorded by the law of nations to such allied or neutral vessels [driven into port by distress] ceases when these vessels, in defiance of the alliance or neutrality of the flag under which they sail, commit acts of hostility. . . .[6]

In discussing the status of members of the Belgian government who had fled to France in the beginning of the World War, the *Tribunal correctionnel* of Havre said:

The rights of inviolability and extraterritoriality accorded in one state to the representatives of another state are, if not expressly defined by statute, prescribed by the traditional usages which are based on the necessity of exempting [these representatives] from the jurisdiction of the state which has received them. . . . The members of the Belgian government, actually domiciled in France, enjoy all these rights of inviolability and extraterritoriality *without the necessity of embodying them in a* [*French*] *law or decree.*[7]

In a number of cases, French courts were urged to interpret article 14 of the civil code as being applicable to suits between French citizens and foreign governments. This the courts refused to do, stating that according to customary international law a state is immune from suit in the courts of another state, and that article 14 of the civil code had not intended to violate this rule of customary international law.

[6] Decision of Sept. 7, 1832; S. 1832. 1. 591.

[7] *Affaire D.*; decision of Nov. 15, 1915; Cl. 1916, 464 (italics inserted).

Article 14 permits French citizens to bring suit in French courts against resident and non-resident foreigners, for the enforcement of obligations arising from contracts concluded in France or abroad.

In the case *Ternaux-Gandolphe* v. *Haiti* the plaintiff had brought suit against Haiti under article 14 of the civil code. The court declared itself incompetent to entertain a suit against a foreign state, and rejected the claim that article 14 applied to suits against foreign states. It said:

A principle sanctioned by the law of nations declares that states are independent of each other. . . . If the contracts entered into by one state be subjected to the jurisdiction of another, the independence of the former would necessarily cease. . . . *This independence* of states which all publicists recognize *has never been contested by France*. . . .[8]

The court then referred to the debates on the civil code during which it was generally agreed that article 14 should not apply to diplomatic representatives accredited in France. The court concluded that if diplomatic representatives were immune from the jurisdiction granted to French courts by article 14, so much more must the governments from whom these representatives derived their position be immune.[9]

This interpretation of article 14 was affirmed by the *Cour de cassation* in the well-known case *Gouvernement espagnol v. Lambège et Pujol.* The Spanish government had made a contract for the delivery of shoes with Lambège & Pujol. When the Spanish government refused to pay for the shoes, Lambège & Pujol garnisheed money owed to Spain by a merchant in Bayonne. The *Tribunal civil* of Bayonne sum-

[8] Decision of May 2, 1828; *Tribunal civil de la Seine*; cited in S. 1849. 1. 85 (italics inserted).

[9] In the same sense, see the following decisions: *Tribunal civil* of Havre; May 25, 1827; cited in D. 1849. 1. 6; S. 1849. 1. 83 (note); *Tribunal civil de la Seine*, April 16, 1847; cited in D. 1849. 1. 7 (note).

moned the Spanish minister of finance, who had refused to honor a draft drawn by the minister of the military treasury of Spain in favor of Lambège & Pujol; the minister of finance refused to appear. The court thereupon ordered that the money owed to Spain by the Bayonne merchant be delivered to Lambège & Pujol, to cover the sum of the unpaid draft. The decision was affirmed by the *Cour d'appel* of Pau on May 6, 1845.[10]

The case was appealed to the *Cour de cassation* on the ground that the lower court had violated a rule of customary international law and had misinterpreted article 14 of the civil code. The *Cour de cassation* reversed the decision of the *Cour d'appel* of Pau and declared itself incompetent to entertain a suit against a foreign government. It said:

The reciprocal independence of states is *one of the most universally recognized principles of international law;* it follows from this principle that a state cannot, by reason of contracts which it concludes, be subjected to the jurisdiction of another state. . . . Although article 14 permits a French citizen to cite before French courts any foreigner who has contracted an obligation towards him, this article nevertheless does not violate the principle of international law, referred to above; it merely deals with contracts between citizens of two states, and not with contracts between a Frenchman and a foreign state; this is proved by the very words of the article and notably by its position in a book of the civil code which deals exclusively with *persons,* and in a chapter which regulates the civil rights of persons only.[11]

10 *Tribunal civil* of Bayonne, decision of March 7, 1844; cited in D. 1849. 1. 7; S. 1849. 1. 87; *Cour d'appel* of Pau, decision of May 6, 1845; cited in D. 1849. 1. 7; S. 1849. 1. 87.

11 Decision of Jan. 22, 1849; D. 1849. 1. 5; S. 1849. 1. 81 (italics inserted). The decision has been followed by the French courts; see, for example: *Cour d'appel* of Nancy, Aug. 31, 1871; D. 1871. 2. 208; *Tribunal civil de la Seine,* April 10, 1888; Cl. 1888, 570; *Cour d'appel* of Paris, April 30, 1912; Cl. 1912, 1165; *Tribunal civil de la Seine,* Dec. 12, 1911, Cl. 1912, 212.

The cases cited show that French courts apply rules of customary international law. In some cases it is stated that the rule applied " has always been acknowledged and followed " in France, or that " it has always been practiced " there, or that " it has never been contested by France ", or that it is a " universally recognized principle of customary international law ". It would seem that French courts require that a rule, to be binding on them, must be either universally recognized or must have received the assent of France; the courts however, have never made a definite statement to that effect.[12]

The courts have interpreted article 14 of the civil code as not having been intended to violate the universally recognized principle of customary international law that states are independent of each other, and are consequently not subject to any foreign jurisdiction. The debates on the civil code clearly indicated that the editors of the code gave this restricted interpretation to article 14. There existed, therefore, no conflict between a French law and a rule of customary international law.

The French decree of Sept. 27, 1914, which prohibited all " commercial relations " with Germans and Austro-Hungarians, has been discussed in the previous chapter.[13] The courts took the view that a rule of customary international law forbade belligerent states to close their courts to enemy nationals, not serving in the armed forces of their adversaries. We have shown that for three generations before the outbreak of the World War, continental European jurisprudence had declared itself in favor of the free access to the courts of private enemy nationals.[14] The French courts

[12] Compare *West Rand Central Gold Mining Co. v. The King*; L. R. [1915] 2 K. B. 391. See *supra*, p. 117.

[13] See *supra*, pp. 150-153.

[14] See *supra*, p. 152.

accepted this view. In the previous chapter we have seen that the French courts regarded article 23 h of the " Regulations " annexed to the Fourth Hague Convention of 1907 as declaratory of this rule of customary international law.[15]

The courts, therefore, had to decide whether the decree of Sept. 27, 1914 violated customary and conventional international law, and, if so, whether they were, nevertheless, bound by it.

A few courts interpreted the decree restrictively and held that it referred to " commercial relations " only and did not close the courts to enemy nationals:

In *Heineken et Vogelsang v. Comptoir Havraise,* the *Cour d'appel* of Rouen discussed the decree of 1914 as follows:

This decree must be restrictively interpreted and not extended to a case which it does not expressly enumerate. Furthermore, even if this extension [of the decree, to include a denial of the right of access to the courts for Germans and Austro-Hungarians] were admitted, it would be contrary to rules of international law and to our civil law to refuse access to courts to a German who is cited by a French plaintiff . . . he would have to be permitted to defend himself (Article 23 h of the " Regulations " annexed to the Fourth Hague Convention of 1907).[16]

The court here seems to intimate that even if the decree actually intended to exclude enemy nationals from the French courts, they would, nevertheless, have to be permitted to defend themselves if sued by a French plaintiff. However, the court came to the conclusion that the decree forbade commercial relations only and did not require courts to declare annulled all contracts with enemy nationals, but permitted them to examine and render decisions on such contracts.

In this case, the court, however, found that Heineken et Vogelsang were an English company and not a German one,

---

[15] See *supra,* p. 153.

[16] Decision of May 17, 1915; Cl. 1915, 1095, 1097.

as had been claimed. Consequently, the decree of 1914 did not apply at all. However, the case is interesting for the light it throws on the attitude of this court towards a conflict between a French decree and international law. The court seems to take the view that the decree must be restrictively interpreted so as not to conflict with international law.

In the case *Geoffroy et Delore v. Compagnie d'assurances maritimes "La Bulgaria" et autres,* the *Cour d'appel* of Paris similarly adopted a restrictive interpretation of the decree of 1914. The defendant in this case was a Bulgarian Company. The court, therefore, had to decide whether this company could be sued in a French court. It said:

Generally speaking the right to appear in court is one of the *natural rights*[17] which the foreigner enjoys in France, apart from any express provision of the law or of any international treaty. Furthermore, article 23 h of the "Regulations" annexed to the Fourth Hague Convention of 1907 declares that in time of war it is prohibited "to declare extinguished, suspended, or unenforceable in a court of law the rights and rights of action of the nationals of the adverse party". . . .[18]

The court then proceeded to discuss the decrees of 1914 and 1915 which prohibited "commercial relations" with enemy nationals. It said:

In interpreting a new law, one must always take into consideration the existing laws and general legal principles which remain in force unless the new law restricts or modifies them in precise

[17] In a note to this case in S. 1920.2.17, Pillet remarks that it is generally known that French courts use alternately the terms *droits naturels* and *droits des gens* when speaking of the rights which foreigners enjoy according to customary international law. The *Cour d'appel* based its decision mainly on customary international law and only incidentally on the Hague Convention.

[18] Decision of April 20, 1916; S. 1920.2.17 (italics inserted). The prohibitions of the decree of Sept. 27, 1914 had been extended to Bulgarians on Nov. 7, 1915.

terms. A decree, enacted under exceptional circumstances, which contravenes these principles must be interpreted *stricto sensu* and care must be taken not to enlarge its terms. . . .[19]

The court found that the decree prohibited only the " execution " of judgments which might benefit the enemy, but did not intend to withdraw from enemy nationals the right to have their disputes settled by a court. The *Cour d'appel,* furthermore, took the view that the engagement of a lawyer was not a " contract " in the sense in which this term was used in the decree. It ended by saying that the decision rendered in this case, by which the Bulgarian company was allowed to be represented in court, in no way violated either general legal principles, or the wartime measures of the government. By restrictively interpreting the decree of 1914, the court avoided a conflict between it and international law.[20]

In several cases the French courts took the view that the decree of 1914 aimed to sever all juridical relations between Frenchmen and enemy aliens and, consequently, did not permit the latter to appear in court or to be represented by counsel. As the courts regarded the right of enemy aliens to

---

[19] S. 1920. 2. 17.

[20] In *Affaire Kovacs v. son mari*, the *Cour d'appel* of Aix held that the decree of 1914 did not prohibit the court to allow a divorce action between two Hungarian nationals (Decision of Oct. 6, 1916; Cl. 1917, 717). The court did not mention international law or the Hague convention, but interpreted the decree according to its obvious "aims"; these were not to prevent the determination of personal rights of enemy nationals. In *Société des Mariniers affréteurs v. Bamberg et Grandoury, séquestre*, the *Tribunal civil* of Épinal also interpreted the decree of 1914 restrictively. This court, however, was not influenced by the consideration that an extensive interpretation of the decree would result in a violation of international law, but was only concerned about the restrictions which such an interpretation would impose on the rights of French citizens to sue foreigners, a right guaranteed in article 14 of the civil code. The court held that the decree limited only the right of enemy nationals to sue Frenchmen, but not that of Frenchmen to sue enemy nationals. (Decision of Aug. 28, 1915, Cl. 1916, 262.)

have access to the courts as a rule of customary and conventional international law, there existed thus a conflict between the decree and international law.[21]

In *Del Prete v. Vulcan Coal Co. et Pourrière, séquestre,* the *Cour d'appel* of Algiers held that enemy aliens were forbidden by the decree of 1914 to appear in court, or to be represented by counsel, but that they could be represented by their sequestrators. It said: " According to a principle of international law, only the belligerent states are enemies and not the citizens of these states. It follows that the nationals of each belligerent have free access to the courts of the enemy state ". . . .[22]

The court then cited the Fourth Hague Convention. It thus found that at the outbreak of the World War customary and conventional international law made it illegal for a belligerent to close its courts to enemy nationals. The court then related that Germany had violated this rule by the enactment of the law of Aug. 7, 1914,[23] and that thereupon France had passed the decree of 1914. It did not comment on the action of the French government, nor did it attempt to defend it as " reprisal ". The court admitted a clear conflict between the decree of September 27, 1914 and international law. The former was held to forbid enemy nationals to appear in court, but they could be represented by their sequestrator. No attempt was made to interpret the decree restrictively; it was applied to the case.

In *Ville de Carpentras, Grisard v. Société Rueck et Cie,* the *Tribunal civil* of Marseilles stated that:

[21] For a discussion of the conflict between the decree of 1914 and article 23h of the Fourth Hague Convention of 1907, see *supra*, pp. 153-156. The courts regarded this article as declaratory of a rule of customary international law.

[22] Decision of July 22, 1915; Cl. 1915, 903. This is a clear statement of the continental European view; see *supra*, p. 152.

[23] As stated in the previous chapter, this law did not violate article 23h of the Fourth Hague Convention; see *supra*, p. 155.

It is true that the principles of international law have, until the outbreak of the present war, prescribed that private rights and their exercise continue in spite of hostilities; it has, moreover, been stipulated in the " Regulations " annexed to the Fourth Hague Convention of 1907 that in case of war [follows text of article 23 h]. . . . But the violation of these principles by Germany immediately after the outbreak of hostilities justifies the letter and the spirit of the decree of Sept. 27, 1914. . . .[24]

The court admitted a conflict between international law and the decree[25] of 1914, but justified the latter as a " reprisal " for violations of the law of nations committed by Germany. As such there are cited the German decree of August 7, 1914, and alleged violations of the laws of war on land, as contained in the Hague Convention, and in customary international war. It is, in fact, stated that " Germany has torn to pieces every treaty or convention which she has ever signed ".[26]

The same arguments are put forward in *Affaire Combal v. Rueck, Grand Hotel de Marseille et Polge de Combret, séquestre*,[27] by the same court, and in *Daude v. Wilmoth et Johann Faber*[28] by the *Tribunal civil de la Seine*. The latter case has been fully discussed in the previous chapter[29] and need not be repeated here.[30]

[24] Decision of Jan. 22, 1915; Cl. 1915, 1120.

[25] The decree was a *décret-loi*; see *supra*, p. 153.

[26] Cl. 1915, 1123.

[27] Decision of March 16, 1916; Cl. 1917, 241.

[28] Decision of May 18, 1916; S. 1920. 2. 20.

[29] See *supra*, pp. 153-156.

[30] The decree of 1914 was also held to deny access to the courts to enemy aliens in the following cases: *Banque de l'Algérie v. Lopez et Cie*, *Tribunal commercial* of Philippeville; Cl. 1915, 669; *Affaire Kaufman, Meyerstein, dit Mandel, Tribunal commercial de la Seine*, Cl. 1917, 238; *Affaire Leo U. et Isaac K., Tribunal civil* of Besancon; Cl. 1917, 248.

The Paris Bar Association (*L'Ordre des avocats à la Cour de Paris*)

It may be well to recall here that the decree of 1914 did not in express terms close French courts to alien enemies. It was passed in execution of the law of August 5, 1914 which authorized the French government to suspend during hostilities the effects of commercial and civil obligations with enemy nationals; it, consequently, prohibited " commercial relations " with the subjects of the Central Powers only. The decree does not state that it is a reprisal for violations of customary and conventional law by Germany and her allies.

Nevertheless, only two courts, the *Cour d'appel* of Rouen and that of Paris,[31] restricted the decree to " commercial relations ", arguing that it would otherwise conflict with international law.[32]   In seven cases [33] the decree was extended to include among " commercial relations " juridical relations also, and held to close French courts to alien enemies.   In some of these cases, the courts declared that at the outbreak of the World War customary and conventional international law forbade belligerents to close their courts to private enemy nationals, but maintained that this rule of international law

passed a resolution on Nov. 30, 1915 (Cl. 1916, 15) which forbade its members to represent alien enemies in court, except by special permission of the *Bâtonnier*. In the view of the members of the Association, the decree of 1914 denied alien enemies access to the French courts.

[31] *Heineken et Vogelsang v. Comptoir Harvaise*, and *Geoffroy et Delore v. Compagnie d'assurances maritimes " La Bulgaria" et autres*. In the first case, the decree was inapplicable, as it was found that appellants were an English company. See *supra*, pp. 180-182.

[32] The two cases, *Affaire Kovacs v. son mari* and *Société des Mariniers affréteurs v. Bamberg* are not of interest for our special problem, as they did not attempt to avoid a conflict between international law and the decree—none of them mentioned international law—but only between article 14 of the civil code and the decree. See *supra*, p. 182.

[33] *Del Prete v. Vulcan Co., Ville de Carpentras, Grisard v. Société Rueck et Cie., Affaire Combal v. Rueck, Daude v. Wilmoth et Johann Faber, Banque de l'Algérie v. Lopez et Cie., Affaire Kaufman, Meyerstein, dit Mandel, Affaire Leo U. et Isaac K.* See *supra*, pp. 183-184.

had been violated by Germany and that, therefore, the decree of 1914 was a justified act of reprisal.

Comparing these decisions with cases cited in the previous chapter dealing with conflicts between treaties and subsequent French laws,[34] we are driven to the conclusion that when a French law [35] conflicts with an existing rule of customary or conventional international law, the courts will usually apply the French law; they will, however, seek to prove that the latter is not actually in conflict with international law. In some cases, the courts have interpreted the French law restrictively and thus given effect to the rule of international law, but these cases are in the minority.

As stated earlier in this chapter, it would seem that French courts require that a rule of customary international law, to be binding on them, must have been universally recognized or recognized by France.[36] Of such a rule it has been said that it " must be respected by the courts as a rule *d'ordre public supérieur* which they must follow and which dominates all the prescriptions of private law ".[37] It has also been said that such rules have legal force in France " without the necessity of embodying them in a law or decree ".[38] Nowhere, however, is it expressly stated whether the courts apply these rules of customary international law as part of French law, in like manner as they apply conventional international law.[39]

It is believed that the answer to this question is to be found in the practice of the *Cour de cassation* with regard to the requirements which must be fulfilled before this court consents to review the decision of a court of appeal.[40]

---

[34] See *supra*, pp. 150-165.

[35] Or a so-called *décret-loi* as, for example, the decree of Sept. 27, 1914.

[36] See *supra*, pp. 179.

[37] *Dientz v. de la Jara*; Cl. 1878, 500. See *supra*, p. 174.

[38] *Affaire D*; Cl. 1916, 464. See *supra*, p. 176.

[39] See *supra*, p. 136.

[40] Compare *supra*, pp. 47-50 on a similar practice in Germany.

The *Cour de cassation* distinguishes violations of French law from violations of foreign law applied in cases of conflict of law. The misinterpretation of a foreign law by a court of appeal is regarded by the *Cour de cassation* as a question of fact only, the argument being that the French court has merely *referred* to the foreign law. The latter has remained foreign; it has not been adopted into French law. As the *Cour de cassation* does not review questions of fact, it has consistently refused to review misinterpretations of foreign laws, by courts of appeal. In *Affaire Seitz* the position of the *Cour de cassation* was stated by the latter as follows: " The *Cour de cassation,* which has been instituted to safeguard the unity of French law through a uniform jurisprudence, does not have the mission to redress the misinterpretation of foreign laws." [41]

The *Cour de cassation* regards the rules of conflict of law as part of French law and will, therefore, review cases where foreign laws have been misapplied by the courts of appeal.[42] It furthermore regards the laws of territories which have been annexed to France,[43] and the laws of natives in French colonies which have been recognized and promulgated by French decrees,[44] as part of French law and, therefore, subject to its review.

[41] S. 1861. 1. 722.

[42] The distinction is between misinterpretation of foreign laws—not subject to review — and misapplication of foreign laws — which is, in fact, a misinterpretation of the rules of conflict of law and therefore, subject to review (compare German practice, *supra*, pp. 47-48.) See cases cited in Lapradelle et Niboyet, *Répertoire de droit international* (Paris, 1928-1929), under " *Cassation* ".

[43] Such as, for example, those of Nice and Savoy; see decisions in S. 1882. 1. 174 and S. 1884. 1. 25; as to those of Alsace-Lorraine, consult Lapradelle et Niboyet, *op. cit.,* under " *Alsace-Lorraine* ".

[44] Only the laws of natives which have been recognized by French decrees are regarded as French laws; see the decisions in S. 1869. 1. 289; S. 1873. 1. 333; S. 1877. 1. 75; S. 1879. 1. 107; S. 1916. 1. 44; those that have not

The reasons why the *Cour de cassation* regards the laws of natives of French colonies, which have been recognized by French decrees, as French laws although they were originally foreign laws, were set forth by the solicitor-general in the case *Mavoulaoumalle v. Agamaden-Marécar*. This case was appealed to the *Cour de cassation* from the *Cour d'appel* of Pondicherry on the ground that the latter had misinterpreted the Moslem laws of the natives of Indochina.   The solicitor-general said:

We must, in the first place, admit that the alleged violation of the Moslem law would in this case constitute *a formal infraction of French law*.   The Moslem law, as it is applied in Turkey or other countries not subject to French domination, is a foreign law, and it is an acknowledged principle that the violation of foreign laws cannot be made the basis of an appeal to the *Cour de cassation*.   But the Moslem law, as it is applied in Algeria or in Indochina to French subjects, *is assimilated to French law* by means of laws, decrees and ordinances . . . which state that the natives continue to be governed by the laws of their caste.   To violate the law of these castes amounts to a violation of the laws and decrees which have ordered their application.[45]

The *Cour de cassation* granted the appeal.

It appears that the practice of the *Cour de cassation* has been to make the granting of an appeal dependent on the fact that the lower court had misinterpreted French law proper, or such foreign laws as have been assimilated to French law. Since the *Cour de cassation* has, in a number of cases, reviewed the interpretation by a lower court of questions of customary and conventional international law,[46] we feel justi-

been promulgated by French decrees remain foreign laws; see S. 1889. 1. 69; S. 1897. 1. 33; S. 1915. 1. 111; S. 1925. 1. 228.

[45] S. 1882. 1. 265 (italics inserted).

[46] See, for example, decisions in: S. 1832. 1. 591; S. 1839. 1. 577; S. 1852. 1. 467; S. 1863. 1. 353; S. 1864. 1. 98; S. 1867. 1. 117; S. 1888. 1. 17; D. 1859. 1. 88; S. 1862. 1. 355; D. 1868. 1. 412; Cl. 1875, 191; Cl. 1884, 61; Cl. 1887, 603; Cl. 1897, 559.

fied in asserting that for purposes of appeal, international law is deemed to be part of French law.

The practice of the *Cour de cassation* to regard the interpretation by courts of appeal of foreign law, applied in cases of conflict of law, as questions of fact has been criticized by several French writers.[47] They argue that foreign law, applied by the courts in virtue of a rule of conflict of law, cannot any more be regarded as foreign law, but has been adopted into French law and should therefore be subject to review by the *Cour de cassation*. Inasmuch as their arguments rest on the presumption that a law must have been adopted into French law, in order to be subject to review by the *Cour de cassation,* they are in harmony with our contention, viz. that international law must be regarded as having, for purposes of appeal, become part of French law.

Anzilotti, in speaking of a similar practice of the Italian courts of cassation, says that the courts review questions of international law, because the rules of international law have been transformed into Italian law, and are applied as such by the courts.[48] His approach to the question is to approve

[47] See Niboyet, *Manuel de droit international privé* (Paris, 1928), pp. 479-84; Weiss, *Manuel de droit international privé* (Paris, 1899), p. 300; Colin, article in Cl. 1890, 406 and 794; Lapradelle et Niboyet, *op. cit.,* pp. 152 *et seq.*

For a statement that foreign laws applied by virtue of rules of conflict of law are actually adopted into the law of the land, see Cook, "The logical and legal bases of the conflict of laws", *Yale Law Journal,* vol. 33, pp. 457 *et seq.* In the case *Uravic v. Jarka Co.* (282 U. S. 234) Justice Holmes tersely remarked: "It always is the law of the United States that governs within the jurisdiction of the United States, even when for some special occasion this country adops a foreign law as its own." (282 U. S. 234, 240)

[48] He says: "The violation or wrong application of international law by municipal judges includes necessarily . . . a violation or wrong application of municipal law". (*Il diritto internazionale nei guidizi interni* (Bologna, 1905), pp. 298-313, especially pp. 310-311). This is due to the fact, says Anzilotti, that the judge always applies municipal law, in

the practice of the courts of cassation of Italy and France, because he finds it in harmony with his theory that international law, to be binding on the courts, must have been transformed into municipal law.[49]   Our approach is exactly the opposite: We approve of the theory of Triepel and Anzilotti because it is in harmony with the practice of the courts.

this case, international law which has been transformed by the state into its own municipal law.

[49] He cites Triepel, *Völkerrecht und Landesrecht* with approval.

CHAPTER IV

Conclusions

TREATIES which have received the approval of the legislature and which have been promulgated have force equal to French statutes; they overrule earlier French statutes.

Treaties which have not received the approval of the legislature will, after they have been promulgated, be applied by the courts. When such treaties, however, conflict with earlier French laws, the courts will, as a rule, apply the French law, and endeavor to establish an apparent harmony between treaty and law by interpreting the former strictly. Since 1875 treaties modifying French laws are, as a rule, submitted by the government to the legislature, even in cases where this is not prescribed in the constitution.

When a treaty conflicts with a subsequent French law, the courts will, as a rule, apply the French law, and endeavor to establish an apparent harmony between treaty and law by interpreting the former strictly. Treaties are terminated by the president.

French judicial courts interpret treaties only in cases where private law interests are involved; in cases where public law interests are involved, they ask for an interpretation of the treaty by the government. The government may officially interpret any treaty; such interpretations must be followed by the courts, even in cases where private law interests are involved. The *Conseil d'État* is incompetent to interpret treaties.

The relation between customary international law and French law has never been stated precisely by French courts or writers.   In the light of the practice of the *Cour de cassa-tion* in reviewing decisions of lower courts, and taking the language of the courts in the cases cited on the preceding pages into consideration, we come to the following con-clusions :

Rules of customary international law which have been universally recognized or which have been accepted by France are applied by French courts as part of French law.   Where such rules conflict with French statutes, the court will, as a rule, apply the statutes; they will attempt to prove that no actual conflict exists between the statutes and customary international law.   In some cases, the courts have interpreted the statutes strictly and applied the rule of customary inter-national law, but these are in the minority.

PART IV
BELGIUM

CHAPTER I

INTRODUCTION

No discussion of the relation between international law and municipal law is to be found in Belgian literature, nor has the position of international law in Belgian courts as yet been systematically examined by any Belgian writer. Michon,[1] when stating the requirements of the Belgian constitution for the conclusion of treaties, touches briefly on the question when a treaty becomes obligatory on private persons in Belgium, and enforceable in Belgian courts. Gneist[2] discusses the constitutional requirements for the obligatory force of treaties in Belgian municipal law in a report on article 48 of the Prussian constitution—the article which deals with the conclusion of treaties. With these exceptions, there has been no examination of the position of international law in Belgian courts.

Belgian private and public law has been profoundly influenced by Dutch and French legal concepts. This has been due to the fact that Belgium was occupied by France from October 28, 1792 to April 5, 1793, and was united to France under a single government from October 2, 1795 until it was invaded by the allied armies in 1814. The Congress of Vienna united Belgium and Holland under a Dutch king.

From March 21, 1804 until 1814 French legislation was in

[1] Michon, *Les Traités internationaux devant les chambres* (Paris, 1901), pp. 346-372.

[2] Gneist, *Gutachten über die Auslegung des Paragraph 48*, appendix to E. Meier, *Über den Abschluss von Staatsverträgen* (Leipzig, 1874), pp. 339-368.

force in Belgium, and from August 25, 1815 until September 24, 1830 Dutch laws were applicable to Belgium. The French civil code, the *Code Napoléon,* is, with certain modifications, the civil code of Belgium today. The Belgian constitution of February 25, 1831 shows the influence which French constitutional theories had on the members of the *Congrès national,* the Belgian consitutional assembly which drafted the present constitution. Thus the principle of the separation of powers is the basis of Belgian public law. French influence also accounts for the provisions in the 1831 constitution which deal with the conclusion of treaties.

CHAPTER II

TREATIES

In the first draft of the constitution of 1831 it was provided that " The head of the state concludes treaties of peace, alliance and commerce; he communicates them to the Chambers ".[1] This article was taken over from the fundamental law of the Netherlands of August 24, 1815 (article 58). In the debates of the *Congrès national* representative Trautman introduced an amendment similar to article 50 of the French consular constitution of *22 frim. an* VIII,[2] which reads: " The right to declare war, make peace, and conclude treaties of alliance and commerce belongs to the legislative power ". This amendment was rejected. Representative Van Meenen then proposed an amendment which embodied, in somewhat different form, the underlying principle of the French consular constitution. This was finally accepted. It modified the general powers given to the king in the first paragraph of article 68, where it is stated that he " declares war and concludes treaties of peace, alliance and commerce. He presents them to the Chambers whenever the interest and security of the state permit thereof, accompanying them with suitable communications ", by adding the reservation: " Treaties of commerce and those which might burden the state or bind Belgians individually have no effect until the approval of the Chambers has been obtained ". Although representatives Le Grelle and Lebeau objected to this amendment because of the vagueness of the terms " burden the

[1] Gneist, *op. cit.*, p. 350.
[2] Dec. 13, 1799.

state " and " bind Belgians individually ', it was adopted hastily and without further debate.[3]   Since article 3 of the constitution stated that no alteration of the boundaries of the state, the provinces and the communes could take place except by virtue of a law, it was added to article 68 that: " No cession, no exchange, no acquisition of territory can take place except by virtue of a law.[4]

Article 68 divides treaties into two classes: one which the king has sole authority to conclude, and another which requires legislative approval.   With the exception of the short-lived French consular constitution of 22 *frim. an* VIII, the Belgian constitution was the first to adopt this classification of treaties.   It was copied by a number of European states;[5] indeed, the Belgian constitution was in the last quarter of the 19th century considered a model for constitutional governments.[6]

The classification of treaties in article 68 represents a compromise between two constitutional principles: on the one hand, it is recognized that the conclusion of treaties is essentially an executive function, since a large legislative assembly is not qualified to carry on negotiations with foreign powers; on the other hand, the rising tide of parliamentary government could not tolerate that the king extend his constitutional powers by means of concluding treaties on subjects ordinarily reserved to the legislature,

---

[3] Huyttens, *Discussions du congrès national de Belgique*, Brussels (1844), vol. ii, pp. 76-77; see also Michon, *op. cit.*, pp. 347 *et seq.*

[4] That this clause in article 68 was directly due to article 3 is maintained by Thonissen, *La Constitution belge annotée* (Brussels, 1879), p. 5.

[5] Notably: French constitution of 1875, article 8; Prussian constitution of 1850, article 48; German constitution of 1871, article 11, Austrian constitution of 1867, article 5; Dutch constitution of 1887, article 59; Italian constitution of 1848, article 5.

[6] See Gneist. *op. cit.*, p. 340.

especially that he modify statutes by the mere act of concluding a treaty. The first principle is expressed in the
general power to conclude treaties, given to the king in
article 68. This enables him to negotiate, sign and ratify
all treaties. The second principle is safeguarded by the
clause in article 68 which declares that certain treaties shall
" have no effect " until the approval of the Chambers has
been obtained. This clause immediately raises the question
of the meaning of the words " have no effect ". Do they
refer to the validity of the treaty as an international contract
between Belgium and the other contracting state, or to its
obligatory force in Belgian municipal law?

We have seen that similar clauses in the French and
especially in the German (Imperial) constitution gave rise
to much discussion.[7] Since Belgium was the first state to
adopt ' this clause,[8] it is surprising that Belgian writers
have given no attention to the problems inherent in this
provision of their constitution. Thimus[9] merely states
that the approval of the legislature required by article 68 for
certain treaties refers only to their enforceability within
Belgium, and not to their validity as international contracts,
binding upon Belgium. Non-compliance with the clause
would, therefore, not invalidate the treaty with regard to the
obligation undertaken by Belgium towards the other contracting state, but it would prevent the enforcement of the
treaty within Belgium. This view has been accepted without further examination by Giron[10] and Beltjens.[11]

[7] *Supra*, pp. 27, 130-132.

[8] With the exception of the constitution of 22 *frim. an* VIII of France.

[9] Thimus, *Droit publique* (Liège, 1846), vol. ii, p. 174.

[10] Giron, *Le Droit public en Belgique* (Brussels, 1884).

[11] Beltjens, *La Constitution belge revisée* (Liège, 1894) ; see also:
De Fooz, *Le Droit public administratif belge* (Paris, 1861), vol. i, p. 130.
Michon, *op. cit.*, pp. 350 *et seq.* tries to prove that the assent of the
legislature required in article 68 constitutes a *condicio juris* for the

We have, unfortunately, no official collection of the debates in the Belgian *Congrès national* which would enable us to discover the intentions of the framers of the constitution with respect to the words " have no effect ". *Pandectes belges* has the following to say regarding legislative approval of treaties: "The king can ratify before or after the approval of the legislature has been obtained. In practice, he ratifies after the Chambers have voted the law of approbation *to avoid a possible disagreement between the national representation and himself."* [12] This statement would indicate that legislative approval is not a *condicio juris* for the perfection of treaties in regard to the other contracting state. The fact that the king does ask for legislative approval before ratifying treaties which have no effect without this approval is regarded by *Pandectes belges* as due to practical considerations, and not indicative of a legal obligation.

Before 1890 the king withheld his sanction from the law by which the legislature gave its approval of a treaty, until ratifications had been exchanged. This has led Michon [13] to assert that before 1890 the king asked for legislative approval after ratifying the treaty. As a matter of fact, the law was regularly passed before ratification took place, but appeared in the *Moniteur* at a date subsequent to exchange of ratifications, because the king did not promulgate it earlier. [14] Since 1890, the king sanctions the law of appro-

perfection of the treaty in international law. This is in accord with his general view on the internal effects of treaties, which is contrary to that of Gneist and Laband.

[12] *Pandectes belges*, under " *Convention internationale* ", no. 71 (italics inserted).

[13] Michon, *op. cit.*, pp. 357 *et seq.*

[14] The treaty with Great Britain, ratified Aug. 30, 1862, was approved by the legislature Aug. 13/21, 1862, but the law appears in the *Moniteur* under date of Aug. 31, 1862; the treaty with the U. S., ratified June 11, 1875, was approved June 1/3, 1875 and published June 14, 1875; the treaty

bation before exchanging ratifications.[15] The law of approval does not authorize the king to ratify, but states that the treaty shall be given full effect (*sortira son plein et entier effet*).[16]

From what has been said above it appears that article 68 does not make the approval of the Chambers a *condicio juris* for the ratification of the treaties specially enumerated, i.e. for their perfection in international law. In practice, however, this approval has regularly been obtained before ratification. Consequently no case has as yet arisen where the execution of a treaty was prevented by the legislature.

As to which treaties require legislative approval, Thonissen and Michon [17] hold that treaties of peace require such approval only when they burden the state financially, or when they provide for territorial changes, or bind Belgians individually.[18] Michon and Thonissen [19] claim that treaties

with Spain, ratified July 23, 1878, was approved May 16/19, 1878, published July 25, 1878 (Lanckman, *Traités de commerce et de navigation entre la Belgique et les pays étrangers* (Brussels, 1883), pp. 189, 131, 111. See also *ibid.*, pp. 9, 21, 51, 68, 267, 295 and 318).

[15] See treaties with Greece of May 25, 1895; Mexico, June 7, 1895, Japan, June 22, 1896; Germany, June 22, 1904; Austria-Hungary, February 12, 1906, Serbia, April 24, 1907 (Busschere, *Code des traités et arrangements internationaux intéressant la Belgique* (Brussels, 1896-97), vol. ii, pp. 241, 289, 270, 581; *Recueil des traités et conventions concernant le royaume de Belgique* (Brussels, 1850), vol. xx, pp. 48, 187, 628). For other important treaties of commerce concluded since 1890 in which this procedure has been followed: Busschere, *op. cit.*, vol. ii, pp. 146, 191, 206, 302, 415.

[16] The formula employed is the following: " Law, approving the treaty concluded on . . . between Belgium and . . . " Leopold etc. The Chambers having given their approval, we sanction what follows: The treaty concluded on . . . between Belgium and . . . shall be given full effect. " We promulgate the above law and order the seal of the state to be affixed thereto and its publication in the *Moniteur* ". (Follows text of treaty and note of date when ratification were exchanged.)

[17] Thonissen, *op. cit.*, vol. i, p. 221; Michon, *op. cit.*, p. 363.

[18] The treaty of peace with the Netherlands of 1839 was concluded

of alliance also may be concluded by the king alone unless they burden the state or bind Belgians individually.

Article 68 states quite generally that treaties of commerce must be submitted to the Chambers. In October 1839 Belgium concluded with the Bey of Tunis a "treaty of friendship, commerce and navigation". The king exchanged ratifications and merely informed the Chambers that he had concluded this treaty. In defending this action before the Senate, the minister of foreign affairs argued that the clause of article 68, requiring legislative approval for treaties of commerce, must be interpreted restrictively and applied only to real treaties of commerce. Despite its name the treaty in question did not contain commercial matters, with the exception of the right guaranteed by the Bey of Tunis that Belgians should be permitted to freely enter and travel in Tunis, a right which, the minister said, was one of those recognized in civilized countries without the necessity of a treaty. The Senate concurred with his opinion.[20]

The term "burden the state" has been interpreted to mean financial burdens only.[21] The term "bind Belgians individually" has been given a very wide meaning. It includes all treaties which exercise an influence on the enjoyment of their rights by Belgians, those that declare executory in Belgium condemnations of Belgians in foreign tribunals,

by the king under the authority of a law passed by the Chambers, giving him full powers to make any arrangements which he might deem beneficial for the country (see Thonissen, *op. cit.*, p. 5). The Treaty of Versailles received the approval of the Chambers, as it added territory to Belgium and contained provisions binding Belgians individually (see P. 1925. 1. 101; *infra*, p. 210).

[19] Michon, *op. cit.*, pp. 364-365; Thonissen, *op. cit.*, p. 221.

[20] *Moniteur*, Dec. 14, 1840.

[21] See Michon, *op. cit.*, p. 368 where he cites statements made in the *Congrès national* to that effect. The treaty of July 3, 1890 with the Congo, relative to a loan to be made by Belgium, was given legislative approval (Busschere, *op. cit.*, vol. i, pp. 290-291).

those that permit foreign corporations to sue in Belgian courts, and finally all that modify existing Belgian legislation.[22] What interests us here most is that no treaty can modify existing legislation unless it has received legislative approval. *Pandectes belges* say on this point:

It is certain that the approval of the Chambers is always required when a treaty modifies a law passed by the legislative power. The chief executive is bound by these laws. This is formally expressed in article 78 of the constitution. The treaty with Spain of 1871 was, therefore, approved by the Chambers because it modified article 4 of the law of April 17, 1865.[23]

Treaties providing for territorial changes must be approved by a law. Thus the boundary agreements with France of March 15, 1893 and April 12, 1905, and with the Netherlands of January 11, 1892 were approved by law.[24] The treaty by which the Congo was annexed, which was signed November 28, 1907, was approved by the law of October 28, 1908.[25]

It is evident that but few types of treaties remain which may be concluded by the king on his sole responsibility.[26]

[22] See Michon, *op. cit.*, pp. 369-370; Beltjens, *op. cit.*, p. 402.

[23] *Pandectes belges*, under "*Convention internationale*", no. 91.

[24] *Recueil des traités et conventions concernant le royaume de Belgique*, vol. xx, p. 324.

[25] *Recueil des traités et conventions concernant le royaume de Belgique*, vol. xx, p. 267.

[26] The countersignature of a minister is required for every act of the king. Treaties concluded without legislative approval are usually published in the *Journal official*. In a number of cases, the Chambers have authorized the king by law to conclude treaties on specific matters, stating that they give their approval in advance. See the law of Jan. 5, 1855, authorizing the king to conclude treaties for the restitution of deserting seamen (Busschere, *op. cit.*, vol. ii, p. 404); that of March 15, 1874, authorizing him to conclude treaties of extradition (Busschere, *op. cit.*, vol. i, pp. 575, 578; Moore, *On Extradition* (Boston, 1891), vol. i, pp. 705, 708); the law of Apr. 1, 1879, authorizing him to con-

Possibly treaties of peace and alliance which do not burden the state or bind Belgians individually, and purely political agreements, as well as treaties of amity, not containing commercial clauses, could be cited as instances where the king need not ask for legislative approval. Obviously such treaties are unlikely to come before the courts in private litigations. They are not of special interest to us. It may be noted, however, that the courts will not enforce them if they modify a Belgian law.

In order to be binding on individuals and on the courts, treaties must be published. *Pandectes belges* says:

The publication of treaties is unnecessary between the contracting parties, but with regard to the citizens of each state, it is indispensable, in view of article 129 of the constitution, as they must be informed of the obligations which are imposed on them.[27]

Treaties which have received legislative approval are promulgated and published in the *Moniteur,* together with the law of approval, in the same manner as statutes are promulgated. No question arises as to their legal force within Belgium; they are considered to be Belgian laws.

In *Verdi v. Stoumon, Calabresi et Esardier* the *Tribunal civil* of Brussels applied the Franco-Belgian treaties on artistic and literary property of 1852, 1861, 1873 and 1879, stating:

By the terms of article 68 of the constitution " the treaties of commerce and those which might burden the state or bind

clude treaties for the protection of trade marks (Busschere, *op. cit.,* vol. ii, p. 481), etc. When publishing these treaties, the law is also published.

[27] *Pandectes belges,* under *"Convention internationale,"* no. 137. Articles 69 and 129 of the Belgian constitution declare that laws are only obligatory after promulgation and publication, and decrees after publication. See also laws of Feb. 28, 1845 and Dec. 23, 1865 prescribing the formula for promulgation.

Belgians individually have no effect until the approval of the Chambers has been obtained "; *this sanction results in ranging them among the Belgian laws,* they must, *therefore,* be applied and interpreted by the courts exactly like the laws themselves.[28]

In *De Ridder-Tartarin et consorts* v. *le Procureur du Roi* the *Cour de cassation* said, with respect to the Third Hague Convention of 1907, which had received the approval of the Belgian Chambers on May 25–August 8, 1910:

The Belgian law of May 25-Aug. 8, 1910, by which the Chambers gave their assent to the treaty, contains, at the same time, the formal order that the convention take full effect within Belgium; the provisions of article 43 [of the convention] must, therefore, be observed . . . *solely* because a Belgian law prescribes them. . . .[29]

and later:

The treaty of 1907, for which the assent of the Chambers has been obtained and which has been promulgated in Belgium, *has there the force of a law,* and must *for this reason* be applied by the courts.[30]

The question whether promulgation and publication are required to render a treaty enforceable in the courts is, as *Pandectes belges* say, of interest " only for the very few treaties which need not obtain the approval of the Chambers, since, as a general rule, treaties are approved by them by means of a law which is itself promulgated in accordance with the rules pertaining to the promulgation of laws ".[31]

[28] Decision of Aug. 3, 1880 (italics inserted); *Belgique Judiciaire* (1880), p. 1057. The *Tribunal civil* is a court of first instance.

[29] [30] Decision of May 20, 1916 (italics inserted); Cl. 1920, 725; *Journal des tribunaux de Bruxelles,* Nov. 2, 1919, no. 6277. The *Cour de cassation* is the highest Belgian court (constitution, article 95); it sits at Brussels. It is composed of 15 councilors and a president, appointed for life by the king. It is divided into a civil and a criminal chamber. It reviews questions of law only.

[31] *Pandectes belges,* under " *Traité international* ", no. 136, see *supra,* p. 204.

Where the treaty itself stipulates that it shall come into effect at a certain time subsequent to the *procès-verbal* of the deposit of ratifications by a prescribed number of signatory states, it is not sufficient that the treaty and the law approving it be published; the date of the *procès-verbal* must also be published.   So held in *Markiewiez* v. *de Cleroq.*

The case depended on the question whether a German had to furnish the *cautio judicatum solvi* or whether he could benefit by the Hague Treaty of 1897 which abolished the *cautio judicatum solvi* for subjects of the contracting states.   Treaty and law of approval had been published in the *Moniteur.*   The treaty stipulated however, that it should not come into force until 4 weeks after the date of the *procès-verbal* of the deposit of ratifications, which should take place after the majority of states had ratified.

The *Tribunal civil* of Ghent declared that the treaty did not become obligatory on Belgian courts, before the date of the *procès-verbal* of the deposit of ratifications had been published in the *Moniteur.*   It refused to apply the treaty stating:

A law and the treaties approved by it cannot be obligatory [on the courts and citizens] before they have been published, in a manner which makes it possible for those who are to be bound by them to take cognizance of their provisions.[32]

This decision was reversed by the *Cour de cassation.*[32a] The *Cour de cassation* agreed with the lower court that the treaty could not be enforced by Belgian courts before the date of the *procès-verbal* of the deposit of ratifications had been published in the *Moniteur.*   It held, however, that the publication in the *Moniteur* of a statement of the minister of foreign affairs, to the effect that ratifications had been

[32] Decision of Jan. 17, 1900, *Pandectes périodiques* (1900), p. 171.

[32a] Decision of Nov. 19, 1900; P. 1901. 1. 53.

deposited, constituted sufficient publication, and that the treaty was, therefore, obligatory on the courts.

Publication is evidently indispensable to make a treaty enforceable in Belgian courts.

Treaties which have not received legislative approval are not promulgated, as their execution within Belgium is ordered by a royal decree, and decrees are not promulgated in Belgium.[33] They must, however, be published to become obligatory on courts and citizens. Upon publication they will be enforced by the courts. The *Tribunal civil* of Ghent said on this point:

The political treaties which are concluded by the king within his constitutional powers . . . are obligatory on the citizens as soon as they can be deemed to have taken cognizance of them through the publication of the treaties in the *Journal Officiel*. The law does not prescribe any other formalities.[34]

Such treaties will not, however, be applied by the courts if they purport to modify the law. They are regarded as equivalent to royal decrees and subject to articles 78 and 107 of the constitution.[35]

In *L'Administration des douanes et le procureur général* v. *De Baere* the *Cour de cassation* stated that treaties concluded without legislative approval could not modify rights guaranteed to the citizens by the law: " In order to restrain their [the citizens'] rights, the intervention of the legislative power is necessary. . . . The king cannot violate the law by

[33] *Pandectes belges*, under " *Convention internationale* ", no. 140, see *supra*, p. 204.

[34] *Affaire D.*, decision of June 9, 1847; *Belgique Judiciaire* (1848), p. 983; P. 1848. 3. 411.

[35] Article 78 renders the king subject to the law, and article 107 prescribes that the courts shall apply royal decrees only when they conform to the law. See Leclercq, *Un Chapitre du droit constitutionnel des belges* (Brussels, 1853), p. 31.

making treaties. Laws can only be modified if the legislature has intervened to render such treaties valid." [36] Nor will treaties concluded by the king alone be enforced unless they have been published. The *Tribunal civil* of Ghent said with regard to an unpublished treaty: " It is obligatory between the contracting states upon ratification, but it cannot subject private persons to the payment of penalties for facts and in pursuance of conventions of which they have no cognizance." [37]

It is evident from the cases cited above that Belgian courts apply treaties because they regard them as having the force of laws or of royal decrees, and on condition that they have been published.[38]

Treaties which have received legislative approval overrule previous Belgian statute law. The *Tribunal de commerce* of Antwerp stated on September 27, 1901:

In Belgium Frenchmen can no longer be subjected to the exceptional provisions of article 53 of the Belgian law of March 25, 1876, because they are, in accordance with article 1 of the Franco-Belgian treaty of July 8, 1899, which has obtained force of law in Belgium on August 25, 1900, governed by the same rules of competence as Belgians; the parties must submit to the *new law.*[39]

With respect to the same treaty, the *Tribunal civil* of Mons said that " article 1 of this convention overrules, in fact, with respect to Frenchmen, articles 52 and 53 of the law of

[36] Decision of June 25, 1883; *Belgique Judiciaire* (1883), p. 811.

[37] *L'Administration des douanes et le procureur général v. De Baere,* decision of Jan. 19, 1883; P. 1883. 3. 67.

[38] The exceptional status allowed treaties between sovereigns, in which they stipulate the conditions of royal marriages, will be discussed in connection with the famous case decided by the *Cour de cassation,* Jan. 25, 1906; see *infra,* pp. 219-220.

[39] *Journal des tribunaux* (1901), p. 1100 (italics inserted).

1876 ".[40]   In *Osram Cie.* v. *Procureur général* the *Cour de cassation* held that the Treaty of Versailles had overruled article 10 of the Belgian law of November 10, 1918, which denied German nationals the right to oppose sequestration orders in the Belgian courts.   It said: " Article 10 of the law of November 10, 1918 . . . cannot be invoked, as opposing the jurisdiction of this court; the law of 1918 contained war measures which have, in certain respects, been superseded by the Treaty of Versailles. . . ." [41]

As has been stated already, only treaties which have received legislative approval can overrule Belgian statutes.[42] Treaties which are concluded by the king alone have the force of decrees, and can therefore not overrule existing statutes.   The courts admit that such treaties bind Belgium, but maintain that they cannot be enforced in the courts.[43]

This frank admission by Belgian jurisprudence that only treaties which have been approved by the legislature have force of law in Belgium, and that those concluded by the king alone have force of royal decrees only, prevents the courts from rendering such conflicting decisions as we have observed in France, where the courts were reluctant to permit treaties concluded under the 1852 constitution to modify existing legislation.[44]

No cases have as yet arisen where a Belgian law conflicted with a previous treaty.   In two recent decisions it was argued that a conflict existed between the Treaty of Versailles and certain Belgian statutes.   In both cases, however, the *Cour de cassation* had no difficulty in proving that treaty

[40] Decision of Dec. 19, 1902; *Clément v. Chemin de fer du Nord*; P. 1903. 3. 159.

[41] Decision of Jan. 8, 1925; P. 1925. I. 101 ; see *infra*, pp. 210-211.

[42] *Supra*, p. 203.

[43] *Supra*, pp. 207-208; *Belgique Judiciarie* (1883), p. 811.

[44] *Supra*, pp. 140-147.

and law did not conflict.   The cases are, nevertheless, cited here, because of the possible inferences to be drawn from certain passages in the decisions; they may give us an indication what to expect of the *Cour de cassation* should it be confronted with an actual conflict between a treaty and a later statute.

In *Osram Cie.* v. *Procureur général* the validity of a sequestration order against a German company, which had been issued after January 10, 1920, was contested.   Article 306 of the Treaty of Versailles, which came into force on January 10, 1920, prohibits new sequestrations of the industrial property of German nationals.   Suit was brought by the German company to have the order of sequestration vacated on the ground that it violated the Treaty of Versailles.

According to the Belgian law of November 17, 1921, sequestration orders could be vacated in certain specified cases only, and in no others.   The sequestration order against Osram Cie. was one of those which, according to the law of 1921, could not be vacated.   The attorney-general urged the court to apply the law of 1921 and to dismiss the suit.

The *Cour de cassation* decided that the law of 1921 was limited to the execution of the provisions of article 297 of the Treaty of Versailles and did not apply to cases governed by article 306 of that treaty.   The present case was governed by article 306 and not by article 297 of the Treaty of Versailles; therefore, the law of 1921 did not apply.

In the course of its decision, the court made the following statement:

The Treaty of Versailles is indeed an international contract, but this contract contains also private law provisions which have, by virtue of their approval by the Chambers, become part of Belgian civil law.   They may, therefore, be invoked by private persons, nationals and foreigners, *provided no other law is opposed thereto.*[45]

Not much weight could be given to this remark alone, since it is not further substantiated by the court. In combination with certain statements made by the same court in the next case, however, it seems to indicate that in a clear conflict the court might feel compelled to apply the later law rather than the treaty.

The case referred to is *Schieble* v. *Procureur général,* which was decided by the *Cour de cassation* on November 26, 1925, shortly after the Osram case. This was a suit instituted by a German national, an inhabitant of the Saar territory, against a sequestration order passed in accordance with the above mentioned Belgian law of November 17, 1921. He claimed that the sequestration order was invalid, because it conflicted with article 297 (b) of the Treaty of Versailles. In this article German nationals who acquire automatically, as a result of the Treaty of Versailles, the nationality of an Allied or Associated Power, are exempted from all measures of liquidation and sequestration. The Belgian law of 1921 re-enacted the exemptions of article 297 (b) of the treaty, but did not include among these privileged classes of German nationals, the inhabitants of the Saar territory. Since the latter could acquire the nationality of an Allied or Associated Power by plebiscite only, they were deemed not to be included among those cited in article 297 (b) of the Treaty of Versailles. The court decided that the possible acquisition of the nationality of an Allied or Associated Power at a future date and by virtue of a plebiscite was not "automatic" in the sense of article 297 (b) of the treaty. It found, therefore, that the Belgian law did not conflict with the Treaty of Versailles. Although the court was, consequently, not asked to decide whether a law passed

[45] P. 1925. I. 101 (italics inserted).

subsequent to a treaty, and modifying the latter, should be applied, it nevertheless made the following statement:

It behoves the Belgian legislator, when he passes laws in execution of international treaties, to judge whether the rules which he adopts conform with the obligations which bind Belgium by treaty; *the courts are not competent to refuse to apply a law for the reason that it is in conflict with these obligations.*[46]

The court seems to regard itself bound by the latest expression of the legislative will. It remains to be seen whether in an actual conflict, the Belgian courts will follow the German and Swiss courts, which interpret statutes with the presumption that no violation of treaty obligations is intended by the legislature, or the French courts, which do not, as a rule, apply this rule of interpretation. Where treaties have not received legislative approval, it seems fairly certain that the courts will apply a later law; they regard such treaties as equivalent to royal decrees, and laws regularly overrule decrees.

It may finally be mentioned that the Belgian courts do not follow the French courts with regard to the interpretation of treaties. As we have said before, practically all treaties which come before the courts have received legislative approval and are regarded as laws. *Pandectes belges* say that since they have become true laws " they must be applied by the courts exactly like ordinary laws ";[47] citing *Verdi v. Stoumon Calabresi et Esardier.* *Pandectes belges* furthermore state that treaties are to be interpreted like ordinary laws.[48]

[46] P. 1926. 1. 76 (italics inserted).

[47] *Pandectes belges*, under " *Convention internationale* ", no. 163.

[48] *Ibid.*, no. 168; see also Haus, *Cour de droit criminel* (Ghent, 1864), no. 496; and cases cited by Appert, " *De l'interpretation des traités diplomatiques au cours d'un procès* ", Cl. 1899, 433.

CHAPTER III

CUSTOMARY INTERNATIONAL LAW

BELGIAN courts have frequently applied rules of customary international law,[1] but like the courts of Imperial

[1] See for example: *Société pour favoriser l'industrie nationale v. Le Syndicat d'amortissement*; *Cour d'appel* of Brussels; P. 1841. 2. 33; *L'État de Perou v. Kreglinger*; *Cour d'appel* of Brussels; P. 1857. 2. 348; *Société de Sclessin v. Deppe*; *Tribunal civil* of Antwerp; P. 1877. 3. 28; *De Bock v. État du Congo*; *Cour d'appel* of Brussels; P. 1891. 2. 419; *État néerlandais v. Société de chemin de fer Liégeois-Limbourgeois*; *Cour d'appel* of Brussels; p. 1902. 2. 162; *Cour de cassation*, P. 1903. 1. 294; *Toebinte et Themis v. Gouvernement des États-Unis*; *Cour d'appel* of Brussels; P. 1920. 2. 122; *État portugais v. Sauvage, Steamers " Lima" et " Pangin" Cour d'appel* of Brussels, P. 1922. 2. 53; *État belge v. Société le Syndicat franco-belge et Société le Syndicat franco-belge v. État anglais*; *Cour d'appel* of Brussels; P. 1923. 2. 89. (All these cases deal with the rules of customary international law regarding the immunity of foreign states in the courts. For the Belgian theory that such immunity must be granted only when the foreign state has acted *jure imperii* see Allen, *The position of foreign states in Belgian courts* (New York, 1929). *Le Procureur du Roi v. Capitaine Wreesman*; *Tribunal correctionnel* of Bruges; Cl. 1914, 1327 (application of the three-mile limit rule by the court). *Drécoll et consorts v. Baron Goffinet, intendant de la liste civile du Roi des Belges, Princesse Louise de Saxe-Coburg et Princesse Stéphanie de Belgique, Comtesse Lonyay*; *Tribunal civil* of Brussels; P. 1904. 3. 151; *Cour d'appel of Brussels*; P. 1905. 2. 65; *Cour de cassation*; P. 1906. 1. 95 (application by the courts of the rule of customary international law that the princes of ruling houses may conclude their marriage contracts in the form of diplomatic treaties).

When the courts grant immunity to foreign diplomats accredited in Belgium, they do not refer to international law, but to the decree of 13 *ventôse an* ii which is in force both in France and in Belgium (dating back to the time when the two countries were united). The decree makes the rule of customary international law that courts shall not take jurisdiction over accredited diplomatic representatives obligatory in Belgium. See, for example, the case of *Procureur général à la Cour de cassation en cause de Raïf-Bey*; *Cour de cassation*; P. 1897. 1. 198.

Germany, Switzerland and France they have rarely indicated why these rules are obligatory on them and on private persons in Belgium. We shall not discuss the cases where rules of customary international law are applied without further comment, but shall review the few cases only which give an indication of the position of rules of customary international law in Belgian courts.

The most important of these is *Drécoll et consorts* v. *Baron Goffinet, intendant de la liste civile du Roi des Belges, Princesse Louise de Saxe-Coburg et Princesse Stéphanie de Belgique, Comtesse Lonyay.*[2] This case aroused considerable interest at the time, both on account of the exalted station of the contestants, King Leopold II of Belgium and his two daughters, and because of the many difficult questions of law decided therein by the Belgian courts. The facts were the following:

King Leopold II, when he was still Duke of Brabant, married Marie-Henriette, Arch-Duchess of Austria, on August 10, August 22, 1853.[3] The marriage contract had been concluded in the form of a treaty, signed by the plenipotentiaries of the two reigning sovereigns of Belgium and Austria respectively; it was not ratified by King Leopold I until September 10, 1853. The treaty stipulated that the properties of husband and wife should remain separated. The Belgian civil code prescribes that property shall be held jointly in marriage, unless a different régime is agreed upon and embodied in a marriage contract, concluded before the marriage takes place, and signed by a notary public. After the death of Queen Marie-Henriette, her two daughters contested the validity of the treaty of 1853. Leaving aside the

---

[2] We shall hereafter refer to this case as the "marriage contract case."

[3] The marriage took place by proxy on Aug. 10, 1853; the royal couple were personally married Aug. 22, 1853.

points of law which do not concern our special problem, the two main arguments against the legality of the treaty were these:

The first contention was that the conclusion of the marriage contract without the signature of a notary public and in the form of a treaty constituted a violation of Belgian civil law.

The second contention was that the treaty of 1853 had been ratified by the king without ministerial countersignature, that it had not received legislative approval, in spite of the fact that its provisions bound Belgians individually, and that it consequently violated article 68 of the constitution.

The validity of the treaty was upheld by the *Tribunal civil* of Brussels,[4] the *Cour d'appel* of Brussels,[5] and finally the *Cour de cassation.*[6]

To the first contention all three courts replied that an ancient usage, which had developed into a rule of customary international law, permitted the princes of royal houses to conclude their marriage contracts in the form of treaties. The *Tribunal civil* of Brussels merely stated that by concluding the marriage contract in the form of a treaty, Belgian civil law had not been modified in substance, but only in form. Since the treaty provided for a marriage régime recognized by the civil code, the court held that the exemption of princes of the royal house from the requirement of the civil code that marriage contracts be signed by a notary public, did not violate the equality guaranteed to all Belgians by the constitution.

[4] Decision of April 20, 1904; P. 1904. 3. 151.

[5] Decision of Feb. 20, 1905; P. 1905. 2. 65. There are three courts of appeal in Belgium, sitting respectively at Brussels, Ghent and Liège. The judges are appointed for life by the king. The courts hear appeals from the tribunals of first instance and the commercial tribunals.

[6] Decision of Jan. 25, 1906; P. 1906. 1. 95.

The *Cour d'appel* of Brussels went into the matter more thoroughly. It related how the usage had grown into a rule of customary international law which was recognized by the first Belgian king who concluded his marriage in the form of a treaty. His plenipotentiary had been a former member of the Belgian *Congrès national*. The court stressed the fact that neither he nor any other member of that assembly had objected to this modification of the civil code. It then cited a number of treaties concluded by various Belgian princes to fix the régime of their marriages, and emphasized the fact that the Chambers had, on the occasion of the conclusion of the marriage treaty of Princess Stéphanie, approved of this practice, and declared it to be in accord with Belgian public law. The court even cited statements of members of the French legislature who had approved of the marriage treaty of Princess Louise of Orleans with King Leopold I of Belgium, and had not regarded it as violating the equality guaranteed to Frenchmen by the French constitution. The court finally stated that the civil code was not modified in substance, but only in form.

The *Cour de cassation* repeated what the *Cour d'appel* had said, but in addition, took great pains to show that the object of the civil code in requiring that marriage contracts should be signed by a notary public was to insure authenticity of these documents, and that this authenticity was equally well obtained by the signature of diplomatic representatives to a treaty. The purely formal modification of the civil code caused by the conclusion of the marriage contract in the form of a treaty did not, in the opinion of the court, in any way modify the rights and interests of the contracting parties. There was thus no inequality before the law.

The manner in which the three courts applied what they felt had from usage developed into a rule of customary international law, is significant. The *Tribunal civil* of

Brussels said of this rule: " Tacitly, but formally accepted by civilized countries, it has, by virtue of the consent of all, become obligatory to the same degree, as if it existed as a written law in the different states."[7] The sole fact that a rule is generally recognized by all civilized states suffices, in the court's opinion, to give it force of law within those states.

The *Cour d'appel* found that the usage of concluding the marriage contracts of reigning princes in the form of treaties had begun in ancient times and " continued to this day in a positive and general manner, so that it has developed into a rule of international law which has as yet never been contested ".[8] When Belgium became an independent state this rule of customary international law was in existence. The court then related how Belgium's first king had concluded his marriage contract in the form of a treaty. This action of the king was approved by the members of the *Congrès national;* it was, at a later date declared to be in conformity with Belgian public law by the members of the legislature.[9] The court found that " this rule, which was henceforth [10] retained by Belgian public law, has since been continually observed ".[11] and cited a number of marriage treaties concluded by Belgian princes and princesses.

Underlying the reasoning of the *Cour d'appel* is the thought that a new state that wishes to enter the family of nations must accept the generally recognized rules of international law existing at the time of its entry. The court

[7] P. 1904. 3. 153.

[8] P. 1905. 2. 87.

[9] P. 1905. 2. 87. The matter was discussed in the Chambers during the debates on a law to provide funds for a dowry promised in the marriage contract of Princess Stéphanie of Belgium.

[10] That is, since the first marriage treaty concluded by Leopold I.

[11] P. 1905. 2. 88.

found that the rule of customary international law that princes of ruling houses may conclude their marriage contracts in the form of diplomatic treaties had been accepted by the Belgian executive and legislature, and that the latter had declared it to be in conformity with Belgian public law. Although the court does not state that this rule of customary international law had been *adopted* into Belgian municipal law, the facts which it relates clearly constitute such an adoption.

The *Cour de cassation* went a step further and definitely said that the rule in question is part of Belgian municipal law. It stated:

The law of nations forms, in different degrees, part of the municipal law of states; this principle is so true that Blackstone has declared that the law of nations, whenever any question arises which is properly the object of its jurisdiction, is in England adopted in its entire extent and is held to be part of the law of the land. And similarly, Thomas Jefferson and Daniel Webster, who both have been secretaries of state of the United States, have attested that the Supreme Court there has placed customary international law in the same rank with conventional international law, and has proclaimed that all federal courts must respect the law of nations as part of the law of the land. *This principle holds with equal force in Belgium.*[12]

The highest Belgian court has thus proclaimed its acceptance of the Anglo-American doctrine that international law is adopted into and forms part of the law of the land. The rule of customary international law in question was one which the court considered to have been in force when Belgium became an independent state. It had been recognized as such by the Belgian executive and legislature. In view of these facts, it was enforced by the court as part of Belgian municipal law, although it formally modified pro-

[12] P. 1906. I. 109 (italics inserted).

visions of the Belgian civil code. The two lower courts, however, apparently considered themselves bound directly by this rule of customary international law.

The second contention against the validity of the treaty was, as we have stated before, that it violated article 68 of the constitution.

In the opinion of the *Tribunal civil* the treaty did not require legislative approval, as it did not impose financial burdens on the state, and did not bind Belgians individually. The court evolved the curious theory that the treaty had been tacitly ratified by the solemnization of the royal marriage, and that the ratification by King Leopold I on September 10, 1853, without the countersignature of a minister, was purely formal. This theory was accepted and repeated by the two higher courts. There has been no other case where a Belgian court has held that a treaty can be ratified " tacitly ", and it is doubted whether this argument in the marriage contract case can be accepted as representing Belgian legal opinion on this question.

In general, the court seemed to feel that the treaty owed its validity to a generally recognized rule of customary international law, rather than to the Belgian constitution.

This view is expressed even more strongly by the *Cour d'appel* which, after finding that the treaty conformed in every way to the requirements of customary international law, concluded that:

Such a treaty which is of a special nature and differs, therefore, from all those enumerated in article 68 of the Belgian constitution, *is a creation of the law of nations,* wherefrom it draws its obligatory force; like all other rules proceeding from this immutable law, *its force is superior to any which the municipal law of states can confer.*[13]

[13] P. 1905. 2. 87 (italics inserted).

This extraordinary statement, which is clearly influenced by naturalist conceptions of the law of nations, was not criticized by the *Cour de cassation*. This may be due to the fact that the *Cour de cassation* erroneously held that the decision of the *Cour d'appel*, to the effect that the contract of August 8, 1853 constituted a valid international treaty, was a question of fact which could not be reviewed by the *Cour de cassation*. The note in Clunet,[14] which discusses this case, severely criticizes the court's view and shows that it was actually a question of law and not one of fact.

To the contention that the marriage treaty violated article 68 of the constitution, the *Cour d'appel* merely replied that the treaty was not governed by article 68, but by international law.

Despite its assertion that on this point the decision of the *Cour d'appel* was final, the *Cour de cassation*, nevertheless, discussed the bearing of article 68 on the treaty. It found that this was a treaty of peace and alliance which the king could conclude without the approval of the Chambers. As to the contention that it bound Belgians individually, the court found that since the treaty provided for a marriage régime recognized by the Belgian civil code, it had not modified the juridic capacity of the contracting parties and did not, therefore, require legislative approval. To the argument that the treaty was invalid, because it had been ratified by King Leopold I without ministerial countersignature, the court answered that a ministerial countersignature had been given for the appointment of a representative who signed the treaty. With regard to the ratification of the treaty, the court repeated the statement of the *Tribunal civil* of Brussels concerning " tacit " ratification.

In contradistinction to the lower courts, the *Cour de cassation* did not recognize the supremacy of customary

14 Cl. 1905, 497 (anonymous).

international law over municipal law in Belgian courts. In every instance it succeeded in proving that the treaty did not violate Belgian law. It admitted that by allowing Belgian princes to conclude their marriage contracts in the form of treaties, a formal modification of the Belgian civil code had been acquiesced in. The court emphasized repeatedly, however, that despite this formal modification of a provision of the code, the object of the latter had been equally well realized by the treaty. Moreover, it did not place the marriage treaty outside the sphere of article 68 of the constitution, but found no difficulty in demonstrating that the treaty was essentially one of peace and alliance, as indeed it did contain a number of political provisions besides the conditions for the marriage.

The naturalist tendency of lower Belgian courts is also expressed in a decision of the *Tribunal civil* of Antwerp in *Société de Sclessin* v. *Deppe*.[15] The suit was brought by a Belgian company against Turkey under article 14 of the civil code, which had been taken over from France.[16] The article permitted Belgians to sue in Belgian courts against foreigners for contracts concluded outside of Belgium. The court related how the legislators of the civil code had emphasized that article 14 did not refer to the representatives of foreign states. From this it concluded that neither did it refer to foreign states which could not be assimilated to private persons. Such an assimilation would, said the court, " be contrary to that primordial principle of the law of nations which declares states to be independent of each other ".[17] Of this principle the court said that it " overruled the rules of the civil law ".[18] The court pointed out that the legis-

[15] Decision of Nov. 11, 1876; P. 1877. 3. 28.

[16] See the discussion of the relation of article 14 to international law in French decision, *supra*, pp. 176-178.

[17] P. 1877. 3. 28.

[18] P. 1877. 3. 28.

lators of the civil code had not intended that it apply to foreign diplomats, from which it was concluded that even less was it intended to apply to the foreign states from which these diplomats derive their position. There was consequently no need for the court to state that international law overruled the civil code. There was no conflict between them.

In an earlier decision, involving the same question (whether article 14 applied to foreign states), the *Cour d'appel* of Brussels took a position in accord with that of the *Cour de cassation* in the marriage contract case. In *Société pour favoriser l'industrie nationale* v. *Syndicat d'amortissement,* the court said:

Foreign nations are governed by the law of nations in their relations with Belgium; the mutual independence of nations and their equality before the law of nations do not allow one of them to impose its particular laws or its courts upon another, for the settlement of differences between them. *The laws of Belgium desire to respect these principles,* whereof a remarkable proof can be found in the *procès-verbal* of the session of July 25, 1801 where the *Conseil d'État* occupied itself with the project of a civil code.[19]

The court referred to the motion of M. Boulay to introduce as article 11 a provision consecrating the rule that diplomatic representatives cannot be adjudged in civil and criminal matters, but which was rejected by reason of its not being pertinent to the civil law, being, instead, governed by international law. The court continued:

The rules of the law of nations which apply to ambassadors, apply with even more reason to the states which they represent. *Nothing warrants the assertion that Belgium wishes to subject foreign states to its tribunals,* especially not by means of article

[19] Decision of Dec. 30, 1840; P. 1841. 2. 33 (italics inserted) .

14 of the civil code which admittedly does not apply to the ambassadors who represent these states. *Such an extraordinary innovation, had it been intended, would have been expressed in clear and precise words,* but cannot be inferred from the above article which, in its natural sense, applies only to private foreigners.[20]

We have here the familiar presumption against the legislature's intent to violate rules of international law. The possibility of a violation of international law by a Belgian statute is, however, not denied. The language of the court seems to indicate that it might occur, but that this would only be admitted if it were clearly and precisely expressed in the statute. The case suggests that in the opinion of the *Cour d'appel* of Brussels, this court would be obliged to enforce a rule which was acknowledged to be contrary to international law.

Whether a rule is actually a generally recognized rule of international law will be determined by the courts. In regard to the principle that foreign states enjoy immunity in the courts the Belgian courts have taken an independent view, and one which apparently was caused by the position of the Belgian state in Belgian public law.[21] Without wishing to discuss at length the Belgian view on the immunity of foreign states in municipal courts, we merely emphasize the fact that the majority of states recognize as a rule of customary international law the principle that one state may not be subjected to the jurisdiction of another, unless it has by acquiring real estate in the territory of the other state, or by tacitly or expressly subjecting itself to the jurisdiction of that state, renounced this immunity. The Belgian courts have, since the decision of the *Cour de cassation* in *État néerlandais v. Société de chemin de fer Liégeois-Limbour-*

[20] P. 1841. 2. 33 (italics inserted).
[21] See Allen, *op. cit.*, p. 11.

geois,[22] consistently denied this immunity when the foreign state acts *jure gestionis,* i.e. not in its sovereign capacity. The unwillingness of the Belgian courts to accept a rule which had been applied in the decisions of nearly all foreign courts who had occasion to apply it,[23] was undoubtedly due to the fact that this rule is in conflict with the spirit of the Belgian constitution, notably article 92.

Previous to the decision of the *Cour de cassation* of November 5, 1920,[24] which extended the competence of the courts even to acts of the Belgian state performed in its sovereign capacity, Belgian courts distinguished between acts of the state performed in its sovereign and in its civil capacity.[25] The former were withdrawn from the cognizance of the courts by reason of the principle of the separation of powers; where, however, the state had acted in the rôle of a private person, the courts considered themselves competent.[26]

The distinction which Belgian public law made between acts *jure gestionis* and *jure imperii* of the Belgian state was applied by the courts to foreign states also. Their theory that foreign states are immune only for acts done *jure ges-*

---

[22] Decision of June 11, 1903; P. 1903. 1. 294.

[23] But since 1886 Italy has not granted immunity in her courts to foreign states, when these states have acted *jure gestionis.* See on this question comments of Professor Diena on Matsuda's Report for the Committee of Experts for the Progressive Codification of International Law (League, Doc. C. 204. M. 78. 1927. V.). See also for Swiss practice, *supra,* pp. 113-114, 117-120.

[24] P. 1920. 1. 193. On this question see Allen, *op. cit.,* p. 11.

[25] Compare with the distinction in French administrative law between acts *jure gestionis* of the French state, which are controlled by the *Conseil d'État* in *actions de pleine juridiction,* and acts *jure imperii,* a limited number of which may be annulled by the *Conseil d'État* in *actions d'annullment,* but of which all *actes de gouvernements* escape judicial control entirely. See *supra,* p. 167.

[26] Cases cited in Allen, *op. cit.,* p. 11.

tionis represents an extension of Belgian constitutional theory into the realm of international law. Although in the majority of states the courts regarded themselves prevented by international law from taking jurisdiction over foreign states—except where these states had submitted to their jurisdiction, tacitly or expressly—Belgian courts denied the existence of such a rule and applied the concepts of Belgian public law to this question of international law. The fact that Belgian courts so readily accepted what was decidedly a minority view regarding the rule of international law, may be taken as an indication of their unwillingness to concede to a rule of international law superiority over Belgian law.

Rules of customary international law are applied by the courts when they are generally recognized and nothing warrants the inference that Belgium wishes to disregard them. In the marriage contract case it was shown that the rule in question had been recognized by the Belgian executive and legislature at the time when Belgium became an independent state and entered the family of nations. Generally recognized rules of customary international law are applied by the courts as part of Belgian law, into which they have been adopted.

CHAPTER IV

CONCLUSIONS

TREATIES which have received the approval of the legislature, and which have been promulgated and published, have force of law and are applied and interpreted by the courts like Belgian laws. Treaties which are concluded by the king without having received the approval of the legislature, and which have been published, have the force of royal decrees and will be applied and interpreted by the courts like royal decrees. All treaties of commerce, and all treaties which might burden the state financially or bind Belgians individually or modify Belgian laws, as well as treaties providing for acquisition, cession or exchange of territory, must receive legislative approval to be binding on the courts.

Treaties which have received the approval of the legislature, and have been promulgated and published, have force at least equal to that of other Belgian laws; they overrule previous laws. It has not been decided whether they can be overruled by a subsequent Belgian law. In two cases the *Cour de Cassation* has manifested a leaning towards declaring itself incompetent to disregard the last expression of the legislative will, in cases of a conflict between treaty and law.

Treaties which have not received the approval of the legislature have, after publication, the force of royal decrees and cannot overrule or modify a Belgian law. They would probably be overruled by a subsequent law, but no case has as yet arisen where a conflict between such a treaty and a later Belgian law existed. Only few treaties are concluded without legislative approval.

226

Generally recognized rules of customary international law are deemed to have been accepted by Belgium unless there is clear proof to the contrary. The courts will determine in each case whether a given rule is a generally recognized rule of customary international law. Such a rule will be applied by the courts as part of Belgian municipal law.

A rule of customary international law which has become part of Belgian law will be applied by the courts, even though it may modify a Belgian statute in form. It would probably be applied even though it modify a Belgian statute in substance, unless there was clear proof that the legislature intended to violate customary international law. Statutes will, however, be interpreted with the presumption that the legislature did not intend to violate generally recognized rules of customary international law.

TABLE OF CASES

GERMANY

BELGIUM

INDEX